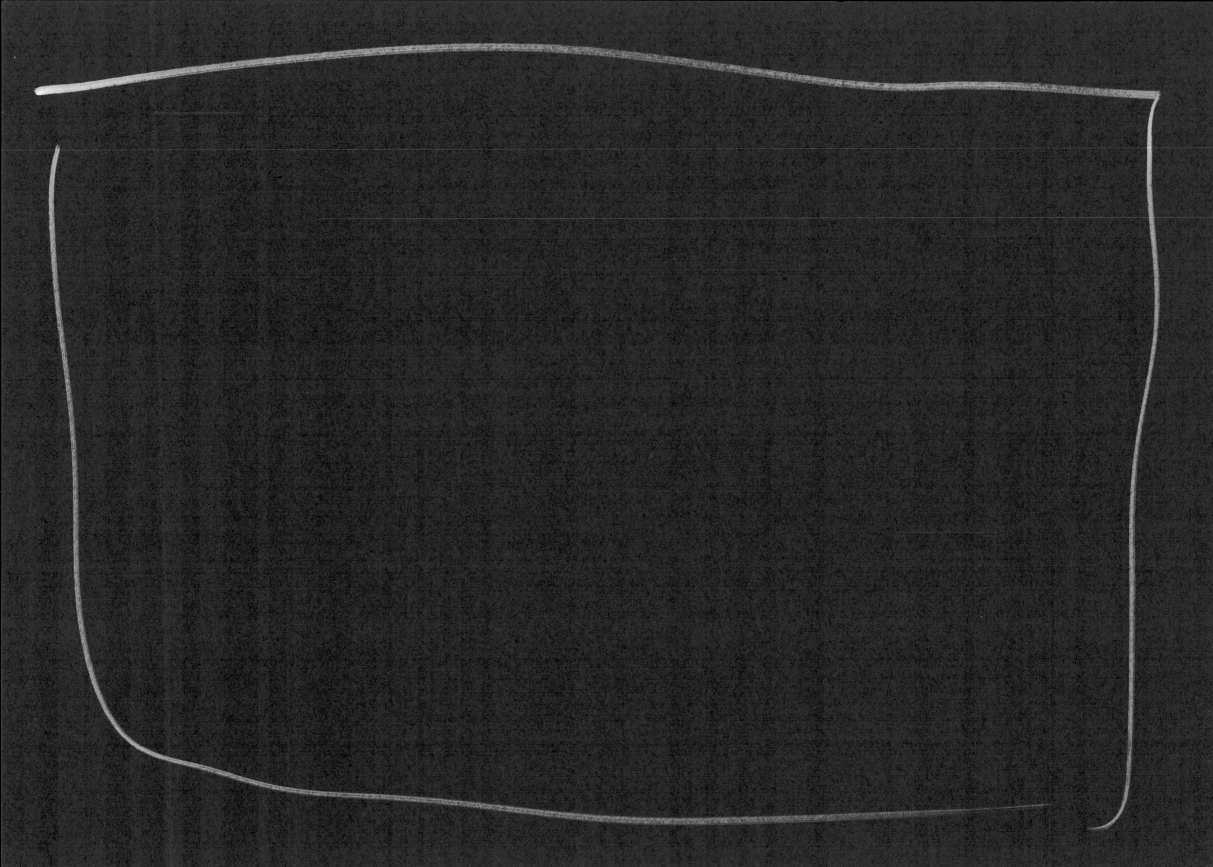

THIS LIVING REEF

THIS

 A PRAIRIE HOUSE/RAPOPORT BOOK

QUADRANGLE/THE NEW YORK TIMES BOOK CO.

LIVING REEF

Introduction, Photographs and Commentary by DOUGLAS FAULKNER

For information, address:
Quadrangle/The New York Times Book Co., 10 East 53 Street,
New York, New York 10022

Manufactured
in the United States of America. Published simultaneously in Canada by
Fitzhenry & Whiteside, Ltd. Toronto.

Library of Congress catalog card number: 73-92293

ISBN 0-8129-0455-9

Portions of this book were published in different
form in OCEANS magazine, Vol. 4, No. 4, 1971.

Grateful acknowledgment
is made to Harcourt Brace Jovanovich Inc., New York
for permission to use the following copyrighted material:
#65 from COMPLETE POEMS 1913-1962 by E.E. Cummings.
Copyright 1923, 1951, 1962 by E.E. Cummings.

#63 from POEMS 1923-1954 by E.E. Cummings.
Copyright 1923, 1951 by E. E. Cummings.

Contents

BELAU GENESIS

From a space capsule moving silently above the luminous blue expanse of the western equatorial Pacific, an astronaut sees a scattering of tiny, jewel-like islands. Hundreds of emerald hills float amid azure shallows, accented by miles of golden reefs extending ninety-seven miles from southwest to northeast. The Belau Islands form the figure of a giant. A Belauan legend tells the story.

Long ago, the island of Ngeaur was alone in the ocean. On a reef nearby there lived a giant clam with a wavy green mantle that glowed in the sunlight. The clam gave birth to a human infant, a girl, who went to live on Ngeaur. She grew to womanhood and gave birth to a son named Uwab. From the first, Uwab's greed set him apart from the other children. He ate more food than anyone else. The more his parents gathered and cooked, the more he desired. By the time he was a few weeks old he had grown larger than either of them. When he was too large to live in his parents' home, a few of the men from the village offered to help his father build a small bai to house the boy. But before the dwelling was completed Uwab had already outgrown it.

Word spread and finally the men of the island began to construct the largest bai possible. Anything larger would not withstand the wind of the great ocean storms. As they worked, Uwab continued to grow. Like all greedy persons, he had a terrible temper. He was always shouting at his parents to bring him fishes, coconuts, and wild pigeons, chickens, lobsters, and taro. Soon there was little food left to Uwab's parents after they fed him. They were tired from overwork and hunger. In desperation they went to the Chief and said, "We come to you in great trouble. Our son is becoming a giant and we can no longer feed him."

The Chief said, "I will ask everyone to help you."

He called the people of Ngeaur together and asked that they feed the growing giant, but Uwab devoured and drank everything they brought to him. Each day he consumed fifty baskets of different foods, drank dozens of basins of water and coconut milk. Still he shouted for more. As he grew, he became so fat that he no longer had the energy to lift the gigantic quantities of food to his mouth. The strongest men took turns feeding him. People came from all over the island to see the spectacle.

It was not long before Uwab was so tall that his mouth was too high above the ground for the tallest men to reach, so they fastened pieces of bamboo together, tied Uwab's food to the tip of the pole, and raised it to his mouth. Every few days the men added another length of bamboo until finally all the strongest men together could not lift the great pole.

When construction was finished on the new bai, the men gathered in front of Uwab and called to him, asking that he lie down and crawl into his home. The giant managed with great difficulty. The men could feed Uwab again but his mouth was still as high above the ground as many palm trees. It seemed hopeless. Uwab grew so rapidly that in no time at all he had to leave his legs outside the bai. After five days only his head fitted under the steep slanting palm roof of the great dwelling. When it rained, and it sometimes rained several times a day, only his head remained dry. Uwab roared his anger.

The people of Ngeaur became frightened and met in the jungle where Uwab could not hear them. They asked the Chief, "What are we going to do? Soon there will be no more fishes and clams in the sea; no more taro and bananas; no more water and coconut milk. If Uwab is not fed, he may stand up and walk around looking for food. In his search he may destroy us and what remains."

The people could think of only one solution. "We must kill him," they said. "Let us all attack him together."

"But we can't get near him with our spears," someone said. "They are too small and Uwab is too dangerous."

"Then let us kill him without being near him," said another. And so it was agreed.

When the sun dived into the sea and gathered the daylight behind it, a gentle darkness came over the island. Uwab soon fell asleep with a hunger in his stomach. Only his forehead rested under the bai. Loud rumbling noises issued from his nose and open mouth. The great roof over Uwab's forehead trembled.

Below, the people of Ngeaur encircled the sleeping Uwab like tiny coconut crabs gathered around the remains of a picnic in times past when there was enough to eat. In the darkness the people trembled and the stars did not sing happiness to them. The bravest of the men climbed to the bai roof, and with strong ropes woven of palm fronds and bark tied Uwab's hair to the heavy beams. Others gathered thousands of pieces of fire wood, piles of dry coconut fronds, and the empty husks of all the coconuts which Uwab had eaten. They placed the pieces around Uwab's outstretched body. Tiny orange lights weaved in and out among the trunks of darkened trees as women cautiously approached Uwab with glowing strips of dried coconut. Quickly they placed the burning fibers on the piles of fronds, wood, and husks. Then everyone stole away, going deep into the jungle to hide.

Around Uwab the little fires ignited others until his outline glowed in the darkness. The light became brighter and brighter, then burst into leaping flames. Uwab awoke in terror. He began to roar and bellow. He tried to stand but couldn't because his hair was tied to the beams. In desperation he kicked his legs and flailed his arms. This only fanned the flames to greater heights. All the husks of the sweet coconuts that had never quenched his thirst flamed in fury and licked along the sides of his body. Suddenly Uwab caught fire. In the darkness of the jungle the people watched in fear and awe. The smoke-filled sky over their island glowed orange, hiding the light of the distant stars.

As Uwab thrashed, the whole island shook. In his death throes Uwab made a final colossal effort to live. He raised himself a little and with one agonizing thrust flung out his arms and legs. They burst into hundreds of pieces, soared into the sky, and fell near and far on the dark ocean.

The people of Ngeaur left the jungle and walked to the shore where they heard distant thunderous noises. As time passed, silence returned to the night and everyone was able to look up and see the stars and starlight on the water. The people danced and sang in their happiness.

When morning came the people awoke and were joyous. They stood up, stretched, walked along the shore. In the distance to the north, they could see some of Uwab's charred remains jutting from the ocean.

Years passed and, in time, coconuts were carried by the currents from Ngeaur to the new islands. Gradually they acquired first one tree and then another until they were clothed with vegetation. Other creatures arrived by way of the wind and the currents. Corals began to grow around them as the fire had grown around Uwab's body. There were clams, fishes, crabs, all the creatures the people needed for food. Seeing this abundance, they decided to live on the other islands. Some people said, "We fed Uwab. Now let him feed us."

When they set sail in their canoes, the people discovered different parts of Uwab's body. Some thought that part of nearby Beliliou was his legs because it was rugged and rocky. Others said no, that Uwab's legs pulled up and kicking are the high land at Imeliik and that Babeldaob, the largest island of Belau, is the trunk of Uwab's massive body. The people of Ngerchelong know that they live on Uwab's stretched-out neck and, to the north, the lovely oval of Ngcheangel is Uwab's submerged head encircled with coral.

The people of Ngiwal, a village on Babeldaob, believe they live in the place that was Uwab's stomach and therefore they have the right to eat seven times a day as compensation for all the food they put there in the beginning.

Some Belauans say that those people living on the islands that are Uwab's legs can run fast and, finally, they say that all the people who live on the part that was Uwab's mouth talk too much.

Thus, with a legend, we begin our exploration of Belau. The legend may be less than scientifically accurate, but on a different level of meaning it is not less valid than the most sophisticated theories of the origin and natural history of these tropical islands. A legend reflects a people's experience accumulated over innumerable generations. Like a jewel, it has facets which give it dimension and life. The legend of Uwab is more than the story of Belau's genesis. Changed conditions alter the lives of all species, including man's. In his struggle to survive, man has evolved in certain ways, conquered natural enemies, migrated over the earth in increasing numbers.

Where he is most abundant he has become very much of a planetary force, eliminating territorial competitors and revolutionizing landscapes, not always with careful thought for his own future well-being.

There are those who would say that some of man's actions are criminal. It is more likely that "moral guilt" is less a factor than certain of his genetically programmed needs that have run riot precisely because he has become so successful. Man is not the first species to supplant others and he will not be the last. Viewed in this light, it is difficult to convict him. However, having evolved in a diverse world, man needs variety. In cities where he has most eliminated diversity in the form of plants and other animals, he has created a multitude of occupations and preoccupations. Yet there are people who search out other forms of life, those willing to suffer discomfort and risk to fulfill their needs in a world that is less competitive—seemingly more benevolent. After the explorers the settlers come, and as industrial man has increasingly migrated to the tropics he has upset the natural reef communities. In a sense, the human species has become the greedy Uwab, with a superhuman appetite, devouring the island Earth.

Primitive peoples worshipped many elements of their lives, and this resulted in a natural conservation of those things which sustained them. The primitive asked permission of the plant, apologized for eating it. A slain animal was honored by the hunter to ensure survival of the animal's spirit. Without honor the spirit would disappear forever. Somehow we have lost this sacred relationship. However, we are no longer ignorant of the damage we are causing our environment. No longer do we ravage the earth unknowingly.

For the moment Belau is a "new world," little touched by the occupations and diversions of industrial man. The reefs and islands have survived many geologic and climatic changes, but they may not be able to sustain the depredations of our unthinking carelessness. This is my only fear in bringing to light this world which I love. If we destroy this living reef, a great beauty and richness will go out of the world, and out of our lives.

THIS LIVING REEF

Belau was born in fire. The ocean floor is not one unified layer, but is composed of massive "tectonic plates" which abut and even override one another at their edges. These giant crustal plates are propelled by movements of the earth's interior, and as they grind against each other bucklings and fissures spill forth torrents of molten rock, forming submarine volcanos. If the vents are large and remain unplugged for a long enough period of time, the outpouring lava will slowly build up through the watery depths until it protrudes above the surface. Eventually the pressure is relieved, the volcano quiets down, and the sea gradually cools the fiery rock.

Eons pass. The restless crust creaks and shifts. In the course of these movements the ocean floor becomes deeper from carrying its immense burden of lava. During this period, organic life, flying through the overlying ocean of air and drifting with the sea currents, encounters this new island and settles in. Chief among these plant and animal immigrants, but by no means the sole contributor to the newly emerging reef, is the stony coral. Living in communities of billions, each polyp secretes a skeleton of calcium carbonate (limestone) upon which other plants and animals build, and they in turn are built upon by others. If the mountain of volcanic rock sinks very slowly back into the sea, the tiny coral polyps keep their superstructure at precisely the right level for their prosperity—within the top 150 feet of the surface. As the reef builds up, its growing mass contributes to the weight of the island base and its continued subsidence. Only the outermost surface of the reef edifice is alive—a thin veneer of life; the limestone interior is compressed, stony, inert. As geologic time passes, the original volcanic rock may come to lie a mile or more beneath the ocean surface, entirely overgrown by a palatial reef structure with nothing seen at the surface but an annular "atoll."

The first scientist to describe this simplest model of the creation of tropical reefs was Charles Darwin in 1837. It remained a theory until 1952 when a group of American geologists drove a hole through layer after ever-more-ancient layer of the limestone reef structure of Eniwetok atoll in the Pacific. The rotary core drill went through 4610 feet, nearly a mile of consolidated reef rock, before the bit finally penetrated the ancient underlying volcanic base.

The Belauan archipelago, with its attendant coral structures, forms a curved strand of volcanic islands and reefs in the western Pacific about 400 miles north of the Equator and 550 miles east of the Philippines. Only a half-dozen of these islands measure more than five miles across. The largest of them, Babeldaob, is roughly ten miles wide by twenty-four miles long at the present-day sea level. The entire group is perched atop an underwater chain of massive mountain peaks, known as the Kyushu Ridge, which extends from Japan southeast to Belau, continuing southwest towards New Guinea. Many of these largely submarine peaks are impressive. The eastern side of the Belauan archipelago drops steeply to the Belau Trench thirty miles to the east where the maximum depth is 27,000 feet. The western flank of the ridge, bordering the Philippine Sea, slopes to a plateau 18,000 feet below the surface some 250 miles away, then, just east of the Philippine Islands, dives abruptly into the awesome deep of the renowned Philippine Trench with depths measured to 34,400 feet.

The system to which the Belau-Kyushu Ridge belongs encircles the whole basin of the Pacific Ocean from the Antarctic clockwise to the Philippines, Japan, the Aleutians, and around to the waters off South America. It is sometimes called the "ring of fire," for it is around these fringes that the earth's crustal plates are undergoing their most dramatic changes. Here the plates confront one another in a colossal interchange. The volcanic phenomena associated with shifts of these plates are numerous and violent.

From the most recent investigations of the major ocean basins, scientists believe that crustal rock is forming continuously. In the Pacific basin the newly formed floor issues from the rift valley as the East Pacific Ridge and migrates westward. At the western rim of the Pacific Plate, the crust dives under the island arcs in the deep trenches. East of Belau, part of the rim of the Pacific Plate plunges under the edge of the Philippine Plate, creating the 27,000-foot-deep Belau Trench. The archipelago of Belau, resting upon the Philippine Plate, owes its very existence to this interchange. Periodic earthquakes all along the "ring of fire" serve as unpleasant reminders to many of the earth's inhabitants that the process of creation is continuous.

The geological history of Belau is actually more complicated than Darwin's straightforward model. At times the crust bearing these islands rose rather than fell; at other times the sea level lowered. During such periods part of the reef-formed limestone that had accumulated on a volcanic base rose above the ocean surface. While some limestone is more resistant than some volcanic rock, much of it is quite porous, enabling rainwater to sink in and percolate back underground to the ocean. In its downward journey the fresh water dissolves the soluble limestone, hollowing out intricate subterranean tunnels and caves. If the structure is sufficiently eaten away, peculiar steep-sided depressions and whole lagoon areas are formed. Raised out of the water, a reef community, of course, dies, but when limestone islands sink again because of continued subsidence, or a rise in sea level due to the melting of the polar icecaps, the reef community gradually re-establishes itself. As this drama is repeated several times over a period of a few million years, the result is a complex geological plot of construction versus destruction, extending through hundreds or thousands of feet, which can be exceedingly difficult for even the most expert geologist to read.

It was over seventy million years ago, long before man walked the earth as "man," that Belau's own story began. Its birth was far more violent than the flaming death of Uwab. A volcanic mountain range pushed upwards through miles of ocean and finally erupted at the surface in deafening explosions of steam and fiery lava. Wandering forms of life quickly arrived even before volcanic activity ceased, and damp black lava beaches became host to a few land plants. The drifting plankton of marine algae and animals settled in the shallows and encrusted the mountain.

Millions of years of volcanic activity continued as other cones erupted from the surface, some rising high up, others emerging only to be eroded by the waves, and still others never quite reaching the surface. When the burning lava exploded from the core of a crater, spilling over the rim and flowing down to the sea, it destroyed the new life in its path. The individual settlers lived a precarious existence. But their kind had learned long before that through vast numbers and dispersal they could weather the storms of a sometimes violent earth. Countless organisms perished beneath the lava flow of Belau's fiery youth, but others followed them, succeeding where their predecessors had failed. The volcanic activity finally ceased. Twenty-five million years ago many more creatures gained a foothold and a more complex community evolved. New niches were available to the more specialized immigrants that could only live in an environment capable of sustaining their particular needs. Plants arrived that lived in association only with certain animals. Animals arrived that fed on the new plants. Other species thrived because they needed a limestone base, rather than lava, on which to settle.

Varying sea level conditions have created three types of coral reef structures: fringing reefs, barrier reefs (including atolls), and patch reefs. All types are interrelated and are found in Belau. Belau's fringing reefs are attached directly to its shores from which they jut into the ocean or lagoon as flat shelves just beneath the surface. The barrier reefs have grown from a previous shoreline that existed at a time when the volcanic land mass was higher and the ancient base of the barrier reef fringed the land. Now the barrier reefs are separated from the islands by lagoons up to twelve miles wide and 130 feet deep. Belau's two small atolls at the northern extreme of the archipelago are barrier reefs in archetypal oval shapes, descendants of the long-expired volcanos. Belau's patch reefs are small scattered reef communities of varied shapes which have formed atop a number of underwater objects, from shallow-water coral boulders to the superstructure of sunken ships resting on the deeper lagoon floors. They vary in size from small newly formed patches to massive mounds that have existed for thousands of years.

At first, fringing reefs edged the islands of Belau except where the rainwater accumulated and ran in rivers to the sea. At these junctions the open-ocean creatures perished in alien conditions of fresh water and sediment but, in time, other organisms colonized these regions. Reefs also formed atop submerged hills that were not far below the surface. The reef animals extracted calcium carbonate from the sea to build their skeletons and shells.

Through the centuries, the islands sank while the reef continued to grow toward the surface and outwards. As a small lagoon formed between reef and land, the reef became a separate barrier. Rapid growth was toward the sea because the river run-off of fresh, sediment-laden water inhibited vigorous coral growth in the lagoons and passes. Only more specialized creatures could inhabit the lagoon side of the reef—creatures which contributed less to the upward growth of the limestone base than did the more active inhabitants of the reef top and front. In time the emerging reefs became the major limestone islands and the outer barrier reefs that encircle the central islands.

Several million years ago, a general uplifting of the entire land mass occurred, accompanied or followed by slight tilting, so that the southern land and reef masses were more elevated than the northern. After this slow process that took place over a period of approximately 1 million years—accompanied by intense rainwater erosion—the remnants of the once-living southern reefs were now high above water. In the next 2 million years, many fluctuations of the sea level caused by the waxing and waning of the polar icecaps resulted in the intricate and varied landscape of islands and reefs we see today.

In Belau's northern region—the low end of the uplift—the small volcanic peak that would become the atoll of Ngcheangel slowly subsided. The fringing reef around its shore grew steadily and, when the central cone finally disappeared beneath the lagoon surface, an oval barrier remained.

South of Ngcheangel, only a few miles distant, Charasech lagoon is encircled with irregularly shaped reef barriers. From the air, or by looking at a map, one might imagine the low crater that must have existed within its spacious center. Now the crater is hidden beneath the lagoon floor, while above there are only the reefs and the passes...silent historians that show us where its ancient shores and rivers ran.

To the south, the wrinkled ribbon of barrier reef flows offshore, paralleling the irregularly scalloped western shores of Babeldaob. Several passes interrupt the reef. The southernmost of these, Towachelmlengui, enters the ocean a little northwest of the partly submerged volcanic caldera of Ngerasech, a name that means "crater" to the Belauans. The large pass (through the barrier) was once the mouth of the river which extended from the crater until the emerging lagoon drowned the river's inner banks. Smaller rivers continue to drain water into the crater from the hills above. The sediment-laden waters flow into the lagoon where the sediment settles to the bottom or finds its way back through Towachelmlengui to the open sea.

South from Towachelmlengui, the barrier reef loops southwest away from the shores of Babeldaob in a long uninterrupted run—all the way to Beliliou, the southernmost island of the central complex. This largely low-lying limestone island sits atop the barrier of which it was once a living part.

The island of Ngeaur (the place of Uwab's death and Belau's mythical birth) is separated from the southern point of Beliliou by slightly more than seven miles of open ocean. It marks the southern tip of the Belauan archipelago just as Ngcheangel's twin atoll, Ngeruangel, keeps its lonely vigil at Belau's northern extremity. Geologists believe part of Ngeaur was once a very small atoll. Reef development formed an ellipse in what is now the northwest part of the island. This tiny ring had a diameter of only 750 yards. Over the centuries the center of the atoll filled with deposits of sediment and later, when uplifting oc-

curred, a raised table-like platform resulted.

The southern end of Beliliou is like the sharp bow of a ship upon which the reef pivots, turning northeast to follow the outward margin of the submerged mountain chain. The small limestone islands atop the barrier and the larger islands within the adjacent lagoon were once reefs capping the submerged volcanic hills before uplifting exposed them. Just north of Ngerchong island, Denges pass represents the first break in the southeastern barrier. From here north, the outer reef is intermittent. At the ocean's surface, the barrier reefs are separated by large gaps because the eastern flank of their volcanic base drops off steeply. Although a reef follows the contour of the mountain ridge in varying depths of 100 to 200 feet or more, its upward extensions are widely spaced. As a result Udel, Eikidelukes, Uchelbeluu, Ngetngod, and Dimes reefs are separated by several miles of open water.

North of Dimes the lagoon ceases at Ngedebaet pass and the barrier becomes a fringing reef. Here the steep-sided Kyushu Ridge is even more precipitous. Consequently only a very narrow fringing reef has colonized Babeldaob's northeastern shore adjacent to Ngerchelong peninsula. Farther north, where the volcanic base is below sea level, the fringing reef becomes a barrier reef separating the calmer waters of the lagoon from the waves of the open Pacific.

Barrier reefs have three distinct zones: the "fore reef," which faces the sea; the top, which is called the "reef crest"; and the "reef flat" or "back reef" facing the lagoon. One zone is dominated by animals while another is dominated by algae. However, the zones grade into one another and many different organisms live in each zone. The factors controlling the growth of all these organisms include water depth, agitation, oxygen, and the supplies of food and nutrient salts. All are interrelated although their importance varies considerably from windward to leeward.

The windward barrier reef front rises from the depths to within some forty feet of the surface where it becomes an upward sloping shelf extending to the edge of the reef crest. Exposed to the prevailing winds, the reef front forms regularly spaced grooves or gullies that run perpendicular to the edge of the reef. Even on calm days the sea swell surges onto the fore reef. As the mass of water rushes back to sea, the undertow combines with the abrasive force of sand and tumbled shells to create grooves. The ridges between the grooves are called "spurs" and are sometimes joined because the corals growing on them roof over the surge channels, forming tunnels. Here coralline algae form the rock surface; they are one of the few organisms, along with burrowing sea urchins and molluscs, that can live in this turbulent environment.

Extending up from the grooves and spurs, a slightly raised smooth band of coralline algae forms a crest at the seaward edge of the reef flat. On windward reefs this algal crest is up to twenty feet wide, the result of strong wave action. Leeward algal crests are narrower because less wave action results in a more diverse community of reef top organisms which restricts the range of the coralline algae. The top of the crest lies at mean sea level and is usually awash at low tide. The outer sloping shelf of the fore reef absorbs most of the energy from incoming waves which exert a force well below the surface. A wave's forward momentum is slowed as it encounters the slope with the result that the wave becomes higher and shorter. As it curls and breaks, its remaining force finally dissipates on the algal crest.

Often storm waves tear loose great blocks and clumps of coral from the outer slope and toss them onto the algal crest, where they are fully exposed at low tide. The barrier and exposed fringing reefs around Belau, including Ngederrak and Uchelbeluu reef, have numerous jagged limestone boulders resting on them. Where the boulders have piled up, as on Mutremdiu point at the southeastern end of Uchelbeluu, they sometimes trap sand and other debris behind them. At Mutremdiu a small sand bar has accumulated behind the barrier of boulders and, in time, may evolve into an island. The four low islands atop the eastern rim of Ngcheangel atoll were created in this manner. During their slow emergence, sea birds, crabs, molluscs, and a host of animals and plants colonized them. Someday, on Uchelbeluu, a high tide will beach a drifting coconut. Other coconuts arrived before this one and were unsuccessful. But this husked seed is another attempt, a chance gamble, to re-enact what was rehearsed and coded in its genes. Soon the beached coconut sends a white root into the sand…and later the sun is witness to a tiny plume of lime-green fronds which take their sustenance from its fire.

Outer reef flats contain a variety of habitats. At places like the barrier reef west of Ulong island, fields of staghorn corals flourish, a rich community sustained by the water flowing through Ngerumekaol pass. The barrier curves inward here and the reef community is sheltered by seaward points, jutting into the Philippine Sea.

Elsewhere, off Macharchar islands, the barrier reef flat of Udel is dominated by dense tufts of brown algae living between the algal crest and a leeward zone of branched corals and small brown thickets of fire coral. This zone is followed by a stretch of sand, then an area of dense turtle grass that surrounds occasional staghorn corals extending to the downward edge of the back reef. Here the reef slopes to the lagoon floor 138 feet below.

Many reef flats are covered by vast areas of sand (composed almost entirely of calcium carbonate), tiny fragmented remains of sea urchin spines, sponge spicules, sea star and coral skeletons, and foraminifera. Much of this has passed through the stomachs and intestines of coral-eating parrotfishes, burrowing sea cucumbers, and worms, and is finally cemented together into larger sand grains. Away from the passes, the back reefs are desert-like compared to reef fronts. The loose surface sand does not provide a suitable base upon which planktonic coral larvae can settle and grow. However, the world of the back reef, like the desert world, contains more than meets the superficial glance. Much is revealed through a microscope or under water to the patient observer. Here is a world of bacteria. Creeping spiral-shelled molluscs hide during the day and emerge at night to feed amidst foot-high volcanos of sand created by worms that pump currents through their U-shaped burrows. Periodic clouds of silt erupt from the crater to settle on the cone, where an occasional sand slide gives the illusion of a miniature lava flow. Safe in its tube, the worm feeds on detritus and organisms in the sand including food which it pumps into its burrow.

The composition of a reef community reflects the vicissitudes in the history of a very ancient mode of life that was quite different in its genesis—2 billion years ago. The first reef-builders were not animals at all, but the simplest of plants—algae—which were able to trap particles of calcium carbonate and consolidate them into laminated limestone formations of considerable size. About 600 million years ago the first reef-building animal emerged, a sponge-like creature that grew in clumps amid the laminated algae. This ancient colonial animal survived for 40 million years, then suddenly, as geological time is measured, died out. Sixty million years elapsed before another reef-building animal appeared. Not one but several animal types emerged along with the progenitor of our present-day crustose coralline algae. This expanding reef community consisted of bryozoans and stony sponges along with the first stony corals. Throughout its history, major environmental changes resulted in extinctions and the gradual withdrawal of the reef ecosystem from sizable sectors of the earth, but new organisms continued to join and evolve within it. This infinitely complex world is composed of single-celled foraminifera, coralline algae, crinoids, sponges, sea urchins, giant clams, and other molluscs (all adding to the bulk of the reef base through contributions of skeletons, shells, and other detritus). They complement the multitude of corals which give the reef its characteristic structure although they may be responsible for only one-tenth of its mass.

The major disruptions of the past that drastically affected the reefs are like evidence in a mystery story. They supply invaluable clues to the tremendous changes in weather and land/ocean relationships occurring on the planet in the past half-billion years. On at least four occasions, the first taking place about 540 million years ago, the distribution of the reef communities around the world narrowed considerably. In the course of these ecological upheavals, hundreds of species of plants and animals became extinct in the brief span of a few million years. For up to tens of millions of years, no reefs at all were built, probably the result of unfavorable changes in the climate, but the exact reasons for this constitute one of the most challenging areas of contemporary research. It is known from scientific data that during the third upheaval, some 225 million years ago, much ocean water was locked up in ice. The shallow seas that had covered the low areas of the continental land masses were completely drained. And we assume that any important change in the intimate association of the oceanic level, the volume of the polar icecaps, and the planetary weather-system which is "energized" by the icecaps (especially the Antarctic icecap) must result in dramatic changes to reef communities everywhere.

When these upheavals happened, many species became extinct but the survivors were joined by emergent species that found the new environment "favorable to their needs." One-hundred-fifteen million years ago (after a pause in reef-building of 20 million years), a previously obscure group of bivalved molluscs, "rudists," began to proliferate. In the next 60 million years they flourished, nearly rivaling the corals as the major reef-builders. Rudists grew in close associations that bore a striking resemblance to coral growth structures since they too consumed plankton and needed a dynamic structure to effect a healthy interchange with the water environment. But when rudists could no longer adapt to or compete in a world of changing conditions they lost their position of prominence and finally died out.

As has been mentioned, the principal reef-builders today are the shallow-water reef corals. These are distinguished from other corals by the presence of symbiotic algae within their inner tissues. In the confines of their ecological niche the algae conduct photosynthesis, using the energy of sunlight for the manufacture of organic compounds. Much of the carbon dioxide, nitrates, and phosphates they need comes from their coral host's metabolism; most of the oxygen they give off is consumed by the coral polyps. The partnership enables the corals to extract calcium carbonate from seawater at a much higher rate than they could do without the algae; it also requires these particular corals to dwell in relatively shallow waters accessible to the minimum level of sunlight necessary for photosynthesis.

The majority of reef corals are colonial. Each polyp is connected by a membranous extension to its neighboring members of the colony. A coral polyp is intricately designed, a cylindrical column crowned by a flower petal cluster of delicate tentacles surrounding a central mouth. Each stony coral polyp lives within a limestone cup called a "calice" which it secretes around its base. When not feeding, the polyp contracts within the calice; when the current increases and its planktonic food is most accessible, the polyp expands and traps food with its tentacles armed with stinging nematocysts. The tentacles transfer the food to the mouth, thence to the stomach where it is digested.

The physical form of a barrier reef, including the life it supports, is determined by the mechanical power of the incoming waves—a result of winds and currents flowing along the island complex. Since each part of the complex is in a different relationship to these forces, a great variety of reef shapes is created. However, the upper surface of any reef front is always precisely at that depth at which the mechanical strength of each living plant and animal can withstand the destructive power of the strongest waves. This is why different plants and animals live in zones, why they have varying shapes and grow to certain sizes.

Outer reef stony corals have more compact, stronger skeletons than many corals living in the lagoons. Outer reefs are host to species which rarely exist in the interior lagoons, ones that have adapted to stronger wave action and water currents. Many flexible-bodied sea whips and sea fans populate the outer reef walls where the colonies sway with the surge. Outer reef corals which grow too large may overburden their holdfast or become dislodged by a strong surge and tumble down the slope. If the reef face is a sheer wall, a dislodged colony may drift down in slow motion for minutes or hours before the branched structure crashes into the reef base far below.

In some protected areas, the reef grows rapidly seaward at the surface and actually overhangs the lower reef face. At Ngemelis, bordering Bailechesengel island, The Great Reef is a sheer cliff face to which divers have given the name "wall." Most walls begin forty to 120 feet beneath the surface at the seaward edge of the reef slope where the barrier plunges into the deep. However, The Great Reef is almost unique in that the upper edge of the wall begins just beneath the surface. A diver can actually stand on the reef flat and gaze down or better still, push off from the edge and hover over an immense underwater panorama pulsating with life.

Near the wall, gold and silver butterflyfish dance and turn in the currents—colorful cutouts spinning on the strings of an imaginary mobile. Above, tiny silver halfbeaks swim at the surface, darting here and there as they eat the rich bounty of plankton. In the distance, at the limit of sight, two black-tip sharks patrol a blue infinity of water. Directly below, the wall glows with muted reds of sea whips, their trailing branches adorned with black-lined silver crinoids. Farther down, recesses are colored with splashes of yellow sponges and pink tube corals, while nearby the yellow and violet bodies of Van Gogh fusiliers swim as one, dancing out a silent ballet.

At night, when the sky is a city of stars, the tube corals feed. The gold and silver "butterflies" are asleep amid the intricate branches of large, black-green tube coral colonies. The fusiliers, clothed in their night colors, slumber alone beneath platter corals. Freckled groupers sleep while sea cucumbers rear up and release eggs and sperm in the current. Sea urchins and long-armed sea stars emerge from crevices and caves to feed. Soft-bodied tree corals expand their glassy-pink branches festooned with tiny polyps which snare the plankton swirling along the wall. Myriad black-red squirrelfish hover near the vertical surface, feeding and talking until dawn.

⇌　　⇌　　⇌

The total reef complex of Belau—the outer barriers, the fringing reefs, patch reefs, and the varied communities within the tiny coves and marine lakes—may be thought of as one superorganism. Its cells are the many individual colonies of corals, the plants, molluscs, sea stars, crabs, and fishes. All these living units require a larger circulatory system to nourish them and remove their waste products, like the human body with its system of arteries and veins.

When Belau was young, nearly all the reefs were exposed to the open ocean currents. At that time there were very few "arteries" and "veins"; only an ocean-river that bathed a young reef community. As it evolved, the superorganism became more intricate. The foundation slowly subsided and the reefs grew wherever they encountered nutrient-rich water. They built gradually upward and more rapidly outward, forming large masses that in another age would become limestone islands. Even when the islands were uplifted, a flow of water dissolved passes and sculptured the islands anew. Each time the melting icecaps raised the ocean level and partially drowned the exposed islands, currents found their way between them. The reefs changed the speed and direction of the currents and modified their flow, but were (and still are) watery transformations of the tide and the sunlight.

We know that when Belau was younger and more massive, the fringing reef growth along the shore was interrupted by rivers. After millions of years the rivers, now passes, are far offshore and considerably changed by the reef communities crowding their banks. Towachelmlengui, the large pass west of Babeldaob, cuts deeply through the barrier reef. The river that flowed from the caldera of Ngerasech was large and the crater was the youngest of the many that formed Babeldaob, for its eroded and partially drowned structure still exists today. Compared with the southwestern barrier reef, the barrier at Towachelmlengui nearly hugs the shore of Babeldaob. The original fringing reef probably got a late start here because of the more recent volcanic activity. As Towachelmlengui made the transition from river mouth to pass, it provided the adjacent reefs with an increasing supply of nutrient-rich water. The reefs grew more than a mile along the banks of this "tidal river." The north bank has grown less vigorously. The south reef is wider along the flow of the pass because the current still follows the same general direction of the original river, bathing the back reef with more ocean water.

Today, Towachelmlengui is the major pass connecting the open ocean to the central lagoon. It is nearly 400 yards wide and over 200 feet deep along most of its length. In a sense, Towachelmlengui is in its prime. Most of Belau's other passes are more modest. At Ngcheangel atoll, Ulach pass has a wide entrance that narrows rapidly because its coral banks have grown across the flow of water. Lagoonward, the pass widens again and becomes deeper. The bottom is covered with snow-white sand where, 100 feet beneath the surface, leopard sharks rest and let the incoming current flow through their gills. Farther along, Ulach shallows to fifteen feet in a region of huge *Porites* coral heads—boulders of limestone covered with a membranous sheath of living polyps. The water swirls around them, flowing to and from the shallow lagoon. Given time and the assumption that civilization won't interfere, a reef barrier may close the inner margin of the pass causing the lagoon to fill with sediment. Ulach may become indented like the barrier near Ulong island.

West of Ulong, Ngerumekaol pass is similar to Ulach. Both passes terminate in shallow reefs bordering their lagoons. Ngerumekaol is a long channel through the barrier reef, but the reef's overall structure belies the importance of the channel's length. Ulach, Ngerumekaol, and the shallow sand flats between Ngemelis and Beliliou are the protracted terminal stages of barrier reef passes. Eventually the tide will flow over the top of the reef flat, taking the many paths of least resistance, which will result in a lagoon of increasing shallowness with a raised reef perimeter that effectively diminishes the interchange of water to and from the ocean. Ngeaur has become a table island. In a future age, Ngcheangel may evolve similarly and in a still more remote future much of Belau's southern lagoon may become land. This region already mirrors the adjacent island of Beliliou, which is primarily a level platform with one raised limestone ridge 260 feet high. However, any theorist must contend with that unknown quantity—the sea level, which won't remain constant indefinitely. But for now the passes are thoroughfares supplying the life blood of oxygenated water and nutrients to the reef inhabitants.

In themselves, many of the passes support as large and diverse a population as the seaward face of the barrier reefs, though with subtle differences. For instance, the interior of a pass is generally more protected from the open ocean waves. Consequently corals and other attached reef creatures live closer to the surface here. Many of the passes are much narrower than Towachelmlengui and rarely deeper than sixty feet. Throughout the reef complex including the passes, the tides determine much of the activity. An incoming tide at Towachelmlengui carries a rich cargo of plankton to schooling fishes in the pass. In turn, the fishes are prey to rainbow runners and jacks, while these larger predators are eaten by black-tip sharks. All these animals are more active and aggressive at this time.

Other plankton-feeders like the sea fans, sea whips, leather corals, and gorgonians expand their polyps to snare incoming food. The sponges, ascidians, and giant clams pump water through their bodies, filtering food. Hawksbill turtles often wing by in slow motion like large birds drifting on the wind, riding the current to the lagoons. One moonlit night I saw two large manta rays swimming in the shallow man-made channel at Ngemelis. They hovered in midstream and let the flooding waters bring their planktonic food to them.

In the passes, the many plankton feeders are situated to take best advantage of the currents but, with living space limited, not all the animals can feed effectively on an incoming tide because the lee side of the reef structure receives minimal current. Nevertheless, many plankton feeders live here and, when the tide reverses, they are bathed in the outflow. The animals that were inactive are now busily feeding. Other creatures including ascidians have adapted to living in the recesses of the reef where currents flowing over them are never as strong.

At Ngerumekaol a ridge of reef has grown down the center of the pass. In one area, not far from the mouth of the pass, the sides of the reef form a narrow gully creating a "Venturi" effect that speeds the current. The bottom is scoured clean except for pieces of coral limestone, even though the reef face is rich with luxuriant growth. The compact, rounded coral heads create a drag on the current and its velocity decreases considerably very close to the corals. When the current is strongest, many butterfly and angelfishes glide among the coral heads, keeping to the lee while they examine and daintily eat morsels of coral, algae, or a tiny crustacean hiding there.

In contrast to the maxim that "nobody beautiful ever hurries," a school of silvery turquoise damselfish hovers above a branched coral thicket, swimming against the current. When all is clear, these tiny fish expand into the flooding tide, frantically snatching at plankton. If a nearby predator alarms them, the damselfish collapse into their home like the particles of a star sucked into a "black hole" in space.

⸻ ⸻ ⸻

The lagoons of Belau, surrounded by the outer reefs and interwoven with the central island complex, have a fascinating history. As they evolved over millions of years, the one world of Belau became many. The limestone islands are a marvel of biological and geological evolution, first with the volcanic land mass, followed by the growth of the reefs, and eventually with the uplifting of the entire land mass which took a million years. Throughout the gradual rise, and thereafter, considerable rainwater erosion occurred in the elevated limestone. The present-day topography of the "rock islands" from Ngeruktabel (the largest) to the tiniest mushroom-shaped islet nearby is, to a great extent, the result of the limestone's surface and underground rainwater drainage system.

Prior to their uplift, the living coral hills followed the contours of the volcanic base. As they emerged, their surfaces were newly clothed with plants and trees. Over innumerable generations, the trees grew and died. The decomposing plant tissues produced carbon dioxide gas, much of which remained in the soil. Carbon dioxide was also a component of the overlying atmosphere and readily dissolved in cold rainwater. The falling rain was a weak solution of carbonic acid. When it soaked into the jungle soil more carbon dioxide was absorbed by the water, increasing its acidity. As the solution filtered down into the limestone base, the weathering process of "carbonation" began. The acidic water reacted with the calcium carbonate (the principal compound of limestone), forming calcium bicarbonate. Thirty times more soluble than calcium carbonate, the bicarbonate compound dissolved as the solution percolated through the various masses of limestone. The downflow followed many cracks and other open spaces though less consolidated subterranean regions. Tiny rivers carved out a maze of channels which merged into larger waterways and sculptured caves. Sometimes the roof of a cave collapsed and still the rivulets and streams ate away at the rock. In time, large circular drainage basins were formed. Along their rims, channels were cut by larger streams of water flowing to the sea, forming separate ridges that, given time, would become the many rock islands. The large drainage basins formed side by side and back to back, sharing the ridges that separated them. Dissolution and collapse overcame some ridges and two or more basins merged.

When the million years of uplift followed by a period of rela-

tive stability ceased. Belau was partly drowned by a resumption of subsidence accompanied by periodic elevations of sea level as the polar icecaps melted. When the last rise in sea level began 20,000 years ago, the ocean was 350 to 400 feet lower. The icecaps thawed slowly at first and, at times, increased their mass during brief periods until 10,000 years ago when rapid melting began. During the short span of 4000 years the ocean rose a phenomenal 300 feet. Gradually the melting decreased and during the past 4000 years the sea level has changed little. Ten thousand years ago the highest peak on Ngeruktabel was somewhere around 1200 feet above sea level. When it was surveyed twenty-seven years ago, it measured 686 feet.

Along the shore of Ngerchol island, fifteen feet below sea level, the mouth of a cave opens into Ngederrak lagoon. In the grotto I found large submerged stalactites hanging from the walls and ceiling. These pale wonders could only have formed when much of the cave was above the level of the sea. Now the tide fluctuates to within a few feet of the grotto's ceiling and the small open spaces in its chambers are filled with humid air and numerous tiny tropical "icicles" that descend in the darkness on beads of dissolved limestone.

Ngederrak lagoon is two miles wide by more than four miles long, an amphitheater constructed by plants and animals and sculptured by rain. More than 100 feet of water covers its floor, yet less than 10,000 years ago this drainage basin was entirely above the ocean's surface. More recently, Ngederrak reef was a jungle-covered ridge, its back to the sea, with an eroded central valley and a gully flanking each side. When the ocean level began its steady rise, a new reef invaded the jungle and the two gullies gradually became Kesebekuu and Ngel pass.

West of the island of Ngeruktabel, "The Bait Grounds," with its many high-ridged rock islands, is a much larger drainage basin. Other drainage basins include Macharchar lagoon, Iwayama Bay, and Risong cove. A nautical chart illustrates the islands, reefs, and the submerged topography. Soundings and contour lines show the basins, how islands separate them, how they are bounded by and share submerged reefs, and where drainage channels flowed into larger basins or to the sea.

All the limestone islands, including the cove and marine lake shores, are undercut or "notched" at sea level. In the outer lagoons, a few rock islands are undercut nearly twenty feet, while in some marine lakes the notch is only a few feet deep. The average undercutting is six to nine feet, for when the strength limit of the limestone rock is exceeded the overhang cracks and collapses into the water.

Notching is primarily caused by rainwater erosion, which is further advanced by wind and wave action, the effects of algae, boring sponges, and other intertidal organisms. Since the sea level has risen, older tidal notches have been obliterated by the upward growth of the fringing reefs or buried under marine lake sediment. Only the most recent 4000-year-old notch is visible. All the notches have a zone that is nearly always underwater and one which is at or slightly above the high tide level. Boring sponges and algae have penetrated the marine zone rock. These organisms weaken the limestone and make it more susceptible to wave erosion. However, the notch's deepest penetration is at high tide level where rainwater causes most erosion. The rain, falling on the island, runs down the sheer cliff face and eats away at the outer ceiling of the undercut. Rainwater floating on the surface and wave upsplash also work away at the rock. At night

the fresh-water layer cools slightly, enabling it to absorb more carbon dioxide which increases its acidity. All these elements are agents of erosion. In the open lagoons, the wind and waves counteract whatever lack of erosion there may be due to less rainwater accumulation on the surface. In the more protected coves and marine lakes, greater surface accumulation of fresh water compensates for the absence of wind and waves. The net result is roughly the same—the undercutting of the rocky shorelines.

The distribution of life within the present-day lagoons is determined by any particular reef's nearness to land or the open ocean. The reefs on the east side of the rock islands from Macharchar north along Ngeruktabel to Ngeruptachel and Oreor receive a constant interchange of open ocean water. Currents flow through spacious gaps among the outer reefs, bathing the inshore fringing reefs. Yet these relatively protected communities are able to build profusely to within twelve inches of mean low tide. Many-hued staghorn and other stony and soft corals populate the shallows. These fringing reefs encircle small rock islands and wind their way along shores of the larger islands. Although a reef's upward expansion is limited by the tide level, most growth proceeds horizontally over the talus of the reef slope. Near the surface, the water is clearer and the increased sunlight speeds plant and animal metabolism.

When one enters Kesebekuu ("eel") pass by boat and follows its undulations, the irregular pastel patch reefs of Mekeald lagoon will soon be visible on the left. These patch reefs originated as old limestone hills or were formed atop coral debris. Although typical patch reefs are usually isolated communities, they sometimes evolve into fringing reefs by merging with one another. Eventually they can adjoin an island or in a future age become an island surrounded by fringing reefs.

The interior region of Ngederrak lagoon and the adjoining west lagoon have less exchange of ocean water and the tidal influx has even less effect deeper than sixty feet. Teongel, the large passage leading from Ngederrak to the west lagoon, is bounded by Kuabsngas and Bedulyaus points. The southern fringe of Bedulyaus supports an exuberant community of staghorn, mountain, and finger corals some fifteen feet beneath the surface. Across the waterway, Kuabsngas contrasts markedly. The top of the reef is in twenty-five to thirty feet of water and the shallower zones are not developed to the same degree. Some factors determining this uneven reef distribution are depth, water clarity, and availability of sunlight. The pass area at Kuabsngas is shaded by the high ridge of the point which drops off steeply underwater to the lagoon floor. The greater depth of the reef top, the silty water, and limited sunlight restrict fringing reef coral growth. In contrast, the west reef at Kuabsngas, like the one fringing Bedulyaus, is shallower, broader, and less shaded from sunlight.

The lower limit of most stony coral growth within the lagoons is sixty to sixty-five feet due to increased murkiness. In the west lagoon, the coves, and marine lakes, the water is stratified. Layering is the result of incomplete mixing of rain and salt water. Rain falling on the lagoons tends to float on the surface since fresh water is less dense than seawater. The Bait Grounds of the west lagoon is far removed from the open ocean. The central ridge of Ngeruktabel and the many rock islands shelter this region from strong winds. Surface rainwater accumulation mixes slowly, sinking gradually as it is covered by new layers of rain. The layers alternate in clarity depending on the amount of sediment suspended in them. Some days the surface is murkier than the deeper water and at other times relative clarity extends to depths of thirty to seventy feet. However, the quiet lagoon bottom is usually shrouded with a dense layer of milky water. Hidden beneath this misty fog are worms, sea cucumbers, tiny protozoa, and bacteria—all bottom dwellers that feed on organic detritus raining down from above. As these benthic organisms feed, they convert the organic wastes into raw materials, which in turn are used by the lagoon's photosynthesizing algae.

Scientists call the microscopic protozoa and bacteria "decomposers." Other people have called the bottom sifters "scavengers." The first term implies a kind of strictly utilitarian purpose, but the second word has acquired an odious connotation. For many people, to scavenge is somehow not to earn a living but to live off the wreckage or waste of others. And yet the artist (who is something of a scavenger himself) may wonder at the equity of these terms, especially if he senses the interlocking cycles of life. His special delight is always a matter of his perception—blending all the bits and pieces of his experience. For many people, some sights, sounds, and smells are unpleasant, but these are subjective points of view. Creative people have always been intrigued by the overlooked aspects of everyday life. The inventors of the telescope and microscope wanted to see the details of commonplace objects in which most people took little interest. Through them and their magnifying lenses we have learned to see the universe we inhabit and ourselves more clearly. Without "decomposers" and "scavengers," not only lagoons would stagnate but human society as well.

⇁   ⇁   ⇁

Geologically, no major differences exist between the lagoons (encircled with rock islands) and the coves and marine lakes which are the inner recesses of the lagoons. Northeast Cove (at Ngeruktabel island) is a good example of a larger cove. It is separated from Mekeald lagoon by a series of ridged islands, giving this body of water and others like it a protected character. Even during storms, strong winds do not greatly disturb them. The steep ridges shade the reefs fringing the shores. Although most of the rain falling on the ridges is absorbed, the carbonated solution still finds its way through tunnels and cracks into the cove water. Rainwater on the surface of the coves also contributes to their particular characteristics. The reef communities that populate them are greatly affected by the surrounding jungle. Altogether the coves are links joining the ocean world and the land.

When Belau was uplifted several million years ago, the coves and marine lakes became a part of the landscape. Just as the coves are more interior lagoon regions, the marine lakes are more interior coves. Although the marine lakes are surrounded by land, they connect to the ocean through tunnels which are at or below sea level. Sometimes the roof of a sea-level tunnel is submerged at high tide and exposed during low tide. Although Arch Marine Lake (adjoining Hera's Cove) is a "marine lake" at high tide, its connecting tunnel is sufficiently exposed at low tide to allow a small boat to pass under the curving arch.

Several small coves, including Jellyfish Cove I, once resembled Arch Marine Lake. The eight-foot wide, open waterway leading into Jellyfish Cove I was bridged over until the limestone dissolved and the arch collapsed. Someday the narrow bridge of jungle-covered rock spanning the mouth of Arch Marine Lake will collapse, for the gradual transition from marine lake to cove to lagoon follows the successive stages of rainwater erosion.

The marine lakes were originally deep basins between the limestone ridges. These sink-holes deepened as surface water flowed into them and onward to the ocean through underground drainage tunnels. When the sea level rose considerably during the last 10,000 years some of the sink-hole depressions were drowned and became marine lakes. Water in them is level with the outside ocean and responsive to the tides which flow in and out through their drainage tunnels. Although the lakes accumulate considerable amounts of rainwater, they are basically marine environments. The lakes vary in depth and shape. A large deep basin evolved into a deep marine lake. Highly elevated basins became shallow marine lakes. And some elevated sink-holes were not affected by the raised sea level.

At present there are some two dozen marine lakes in Belau: twelve within Macharchar, six within Ngeruktabel, two within Oreor, and a sprinkling of others within the larger limestone islands. Many more developed into coves or filled in and were overgrown with jungle. Several of the shallower marine lakes dominated by mangrove swamps may someday turn to jungle.

The smallest marine lake is about 100 feet across. Macharchar boasts the largest, a marine lake with an average width of 800 feet, a length of 6000 feet, and depths ranging from 120 to 194 feet, considerably deeper than the outer lagoons. Many of the marine lakes are quite deep since their depressions often correspond to the lagoon drainage basins.

Jellyfish Marine Lake, which is nearly circular, is 600 feet wide and probably more than eighty or ninety feet deep. Its basement tunnels have been replaced by upper drainage tunnels closer to sea level. Near the bottom there is no circulation. The surface water is fresh to brackish followed by a deep middle layer of warm saltwater that abruptly ends at seventy-five feet. The bottom layer, which does not mix with the upper layers, is suddenly colder and very black. Inside the bottom zone, bacteria have exhausted the oxygen and "reduced" the sulfate in the sea water to hydrogen sulfide. The heavy metal salts in the water color it black—a condition characteristic of the more interior marine lakes with deep basins that are separated from the ocean by long winding tunnels. The subdued tidal water reaching the lakes does not circulate into their basins.

Some of the marine lakes in close proximity to the outer lagoons do not have a black bottom layer. The deeper water is increasingly misty and a fog of white silt clouds the bottom. Ascidian Marine Lake (within Ngeruktabel island) has two large sea level tunnels leading directly to a cove bordering Mekeald lagoon. The tunnels are less than 100 feet long and the water exchange through them is rapid, resulting in greater ocean water circulation within the lake.

The reef community in the coves is different from that of the exposed lagoon environments. The shaded shores and a greater concentration of silt resulting from decreased water circulation inhibit the growth of many species of corals and other organisms. But different species have adapted to these murkier, brackish water conditions. Halfbeaks dart beneath the overhanging cliff-face in the shadow of leafy branches of trees that sometimes touch the surface at high water. Maze corals construct their twisting ridges just beneath the low water level. Their eleborate growth-forms utilize the minimal currents and sunlight in their sheltered, shaded world.

Farther down the slope, large, tightly packed bouquets of fluorescent flower corals glow in the dim light. Their winding, needle-sharp skeletons are hidden by velvet flesh of gray and deep green, red, or pale patterns of green and cream. Away from the shaded shores, gray castle corals construct elaborate towers in the sunny mist. Solitary anemone mushroom corals, scattered on the sandy bottom, trap plankton with long, white-tipped tentacles.

Some marine lakes are populated by similar reef communities. Ascidian and Mushroom Coral Marine Lake (with their short connecting tunnels to the lagoons) are not unlike many of the coves. Thorny oysters and fluted clams add color to the slopes with orange and iridescent mantles.

The more secluded marine lakes, separated from the lagoons by wide jungle ridges and long tortuous tunnels, support a limited number of species. These plants and animals are conditioned to brackish mangrove swamp environments receiving large influxes of fresh water. Few species survive the long journey through the tunnels but, among those that have, some adapted differently to their world. In the lagoons and coves, the graceful *Mastigias* jellyfish is equipped with long trailing "clubs" attached to the manubrium below the bell. This jellyfish grows quite large and even a tiny, two-inch creature sports a fully developed arsenal of stinging clubs to trap food or protect itself. In Goby Marine Lake, the same jellyfish pulse through the water in greater concentrations but are usually smaller and their clubs are disproportionately shorter and more slender. Not far away, in Jellyfish Marine Lake, the same jellyfish are even more abundant. In keeping with their increased numbers, they are smaller still and the clubs of even the largest ones are reduced to stubby appendages. In this lake, the jellyfish may have no natural enemies. Large stinging clubs could have been detrimental, instead of an asset, if the jellyfish collided with one another. Evidently they have proliferated as their clubs diminished in size.

Each world of Belau—the outer reefs, passes, lagoons, coves, and marine lakes—has a special meaning for me, arising from my day-to-day experiences more than from any facts, figures, and dates. These green islands and golden reefs are a living experience, an indelible part of my life.

Scientists have told me that a few of their co-workers were reduced to insanity by unsuccessful attempts to place life into neat little compartments. And I have asked myself, how can anyone truthfully divide up the continuum of a reef or a rainbow? We try—but after all the "facts" are gathered, what do we have? In contrast, a living experience is more educational, richer, and far more lasting…the cement which holds life together. Reality will always be an experience that is now.

It is a glorious day, fresh from last night's rain. As my boat skims over the silver-smooth water, I lie on the deck and watch the surface slide beneath me, reflecting the infinite blue sky over Belau. I have experienced many days like this but each new day is a priceless gift.

My friend, John Kochi, is steering. He knows the direction through Iwayama Bay and the maze of rock islands. We cross an open expanse of water and cut through a small pass. The air is filled with the sweet smell of growing vegetation clinging to the sheer face of the island walls. We speed along the channel that parallels the base of one island and head southeast into open water again. The droning sound of the outboard is muted and borne away by a current of air passing over my ears, but I hear the splashing of the white foam below me as it arcs out from the bow of the boat, cascades, dances a moment, and is gone.

The deep blue water shallows to several feet and the bottom is suddenly thick with staghorn and other corals. As I watch, a cobalt sea star passes below, followed by an urchin and a bed of turtle grass. We turn a corner (the southeastern tip of Oreor), cross another expanse of water, and head into a little cove on the eastern side of Oreor where no people live. The jungle surrounds us. When the water becomes too shallow, John stops the outboard and lifts it up; I take the length of bamboo and pole us the remaining distance to shore. A great silence descends on us and we are suddenly in another world.

John deposits me ashore with our gear and then poles back so that the ebbing tide will not ground the boat. I watch as he throws out the anchor and rigs it to prevent the boat from swinging. Then he slips into the water and wades the long way back. We put on our gear. The vegetation is thick and the climb to the marine lake will be steep over coral rocks. I put on a long-sleeved work shirt, pants, and work shoes. John warns me that one of the trees is poisonous to touch so I put on rubber work gloves. Unlike John, I am a stranger to this world.

Finally I put on my aqualung tank and pick up my underwater camera in its canvas carrying case. John carries another air tank and my diving bag. We are ready to make our climb. I look toward the slightly menacing darkness of the jungle in the deep shadow of morning. We begin. Somewhere below us the sea is bound to this secret lake by a winding underground tunnel. The rising and falling tides pump the vital sea fluid in and out as the mother feeds the child in the hidden womb.

The climb is steep and exhausting. Sweat begins to run down my body. My legs are tired and I find it difficult to control my feet which catch on vines and wobble over jagged coral rocks. John has a heavier load, yet he is not as tired as I. He climbs ahead and then waits for me. With each step upward I grunt for a breath of air. I wipe the sweat from my forehead and eyes but my shirt sleeve is already wet. I try not to become too tired.

Everything is damp and the moss-covered rocks are slippery from the night's rain. Crevices are filled with brown decaying leaves saturated with water. We climb over a fallen tree that took energy from the sun, grew, and died. In slow decomposition, it adds its remains to the still-living earth. Here, it seems, nothing ever really dies. This fallen tree's smell is truly the sweetness of living, of everything living.

We finally reach the ridge of the hill and rest before our descent. We straddle another fallen tree to relieve the weight of the aqualung tanks from our backs and legs; my shoulders are sore from the straps and my lungs are working hard. Feeling weak and slightly faint, I lean my head back and look up. Only a patch of sky is visible here and there among the leaves. No shafts of sunlight penetrate; the early morning sun is still too low. I hear the sounds of insects, the sounds of birds, and the pounding of my heart, all surrounded by silence. It is this silence that is always greater then we are. Yet from out of this silence we hear the jungle singing…even in us, in our breathing.

I stand up, taking the weight of the tank on my shoulders, and pick up my camera. We start off again. My legs are still weak and my feet don't go quite where they should. I walk slowly. I steady myself by grasping small trees and vines. Some break, so I test each one before putting my full weight on it. I follow John around a giant coral boulder and we begin our descent. There is no sign of the lake. It lies below, hidden by dense vegetation.

As we descend, the songs of birds greet us. Cicadas hum and hum in rising and falling waves of conversation.

John turns to me and points ahead through the trees to a glint of silver below. A patch of water is visible. We descend still farther and little by little we see more of the water's surface through the leaves and hanging vines. I now see the near shore strewn with jagged coral boulders. My eagerness increases and I quicken my pace to catch up with John. My legs don't agree. I go slowly again. John is in the water, waiting. Finally, I reach him and put down my gear. The lake is perfectly round. Through the trees, about 600 feet away, I see a wall of green—the far shore. John directs my attention to the surface of the water. Just below it are thousands of pulsing jellyfish. I forget my weariness. As I lay out my gear and arrange it, John fashions a clothesline from a young tree and a strip of vine. When he finishes, I hang up the towel I use for drying off the camera housing. All is ready. I wade over the soft mud bottom of the shallows to the edge of what appears to be a steep incline. John takes charge of the camera. He tells me he too would like to photograph. After I put on my fins and mask, he passes the camera to me. I sit down and the buoyancy of the water takes the strain from my shoulders. The water is like a balm, cleaning the sweat away. I sit and feel its coolness…I feel baptized. The sunlight has turned the nearby leaves a golden green while the wall of the far shore is still in blue-green shadow. Out of the peaceful silence two white birds flutter across the mosaic wall of shadowed leaves like butterflies, dipping and climbing in this little circle of a world. Almost unnoticed, a dark thought steals into my consciousness: perhaps this tiny world, hidden away from the outside with its odd collection of life, is a place come to a dead end…a world lost to me.

Yet I sense something beyond my reasoning that affirms its aliveness in all that I see, touch, hear, and feel.

I push off, swimming out into sunlight. Before me are millions of jellyfish pulsing in all directions. They continue on and on out of sight into the darkness below. I swim down through galaxies of them. Many are large, slow, rhythmic pulsers. Others are tiny and rapid. As I descend the water becomes warmer and murkier. Finally the sensation becomes uncomfortable and I swim up until I feel alive. There I hang suspended and look up at the surface. My escaping air bubbles disturb its mirror-smoothness, making the sunlight shimmer as it descends through the water. The myriad jellyfish offer little resistance to the light save what they trap within the tissues of their translucent bodies. They are only a little more substantial than the water which surrounds them, yet each pulsating creature embodies that miraculous organization which is life. Essentially I am not much different, and if they are not unduly bothered by the limits of their little world, why should I be bothered by my knowledge that there are other worlds, both larger and smaller, beyond this one? This tiny circle that contains me and all these phantom creatures is itself contained like a drop of water under the microscope lens of my imagination. If this little world, this drop of water, is without meaning, then the universe is without meaning.

The round blue mirror of the surface opens above me like a birth canal. I float up from the darkness below. Through the lens of my camera I see all these throbbing phantoms. We exist now, as everything in the universe exists now, transcending the clock that ticks away the seconds of individual existence.

I finish photographing these space tumblers dancing out their symphony in silence and sunlight. I return to the surface, stick my head above the water, and spin around, only to discover myself in the center of the lake. I try to determine where I entered. I spin around again but cannot find it. There is only a wall of green. A momentary fear flickers through me. Then I remember John and call to him. His voice answers from behind me. I turn and see the branches of a tree move and I begin swimming. After a minute or two I see John floating on the submerged branches of a denges tree. When I reach the edge of the shallows, he swims over and takes the camera.

Before going ashore, I grasp the root of a tree and remain there for a moment to rest, staring at the network of dark brown, almost black roots. Around them a wisp of disturbed bottom sediment hangs suspended in the water like a ghostly gesture of something living long ago. I see a movement of dark fins as some ancient part of me encounters, in the shallows, the edge of a new world. I pull myself up through the roots of the trees and stand there refreshed from my dive. I no longer feel tired. John offers me a sushi, a rice patty flavored with a delicate blend of sugar and vinegar.

While I work to change the film in my camera, John catches insects and feeds them to a gathering of cardinalfish. He holds the insect in his hand and remains perfectly montionless in the water, perched on the branches of his tree. Slowly the tiny fish approach and nibble at the insect. When John cannot find insects, he feeds the fish bits of fungus stripped from the bark of the trees.

As soon as the film is changed, I put on my gear and enter the water. John interrupts his activities to hand me the camera. We work together easily. For John, it is a pleasant day.

I put my face in the water and push off. Immediately I am greeted by a group of five friendly surgeonfish come to see this strange intruder. They show no fear as they circle. I swim to the right and they follow along the incline. Presently, a mangrove snapper swims up to me and abruptly stops with a forward thrust of his pectoral fins. I see a photograph and change the controls of my camera. Everything is pre-set. The snapper returns and, in a flash of light, the film records the moment of our meeting.

Growing along the incline is a rich blanket of algae. I let myself settle downward and sink into it. A cloud of sediment boils up around me. Cautiously, I inch forward to clearer water. Tiny cardinalfish hover motionless over the greenery while below them miniature brown sea cucumbers rest upon it. My presence disturbs the sea cucumbers and they contract. Spaced out on the carpet, diminutive brown gobies with inquisitive eyes are intent on their daily business of searching for food.

Farther on, a once-green fern leaf turned to autumn rust is resting on the bottom. As the hours go by I lose myself in my work. I come across a tree that once grew at the edge of the lake; now it lies on its side underwater. The bark that once covered it is gone and the bare wood is riddled with holes, the result of numerous teredo worms which are not worms at all but bivalved mollusc borers. Here and there small brown snails are scattered over a surface colored with the delicate pastel blush of slow decay. On my next dive I discover an abstract of flaming colors — brown autumn leaves tangled in a bed of yellow and deep purple sponges and transparent orange ascidians. It is a richly woven tapestry of living and dying.

I turn and swim back along the incline. The tide has fallen in the lake and the level of the water is several feet lower. The sun is high now, almost directly overhead. I continue swimming and return to John, who is alerted to my approach by the sound of my air bubbles escaping at the surface. Charmed by his appearance, I photograph him. It is here that I want to remember John as I know him — a child of the jungle and the sea.

We swim to shore. John takes the camera while I climb onto the mud shallows and remove my gear. I hang my mask and gloves on nearby branches, remove my tank, lean it against a tree, and take off my fins. When I finish changing film I pick up another sushi.

Before returning to the water, I stand a moment and listen. The sunlight filters through the trees, touching a fern here, there a leaf. A slight breeze ripples the surface of the water. Little fish make silent rings on the surface as they feed. A tiny crab in the mud nibbles at my toe and I jump. A pigeon coos and cicadas converse in a humming chorus of countless numbers. The wind stirs the highest branches of the trees and raindrops fall from leaf to leaf. I look up as a leaf falls, sliding from side to side on the air. The deep blue sky is visible among the green community of leaves. John is singing a Belauan song. Tiny mosses secret themselves in the crevices of ancient coral rocks, damp with the smell of rain. The fern is still splashed yellow-green in sunlight, and the hanging vines arc down from the silent trees. Air roots pop their heads a little above the surface of the water while trees cradle ferns in their branches. A tiny cardinal honey-eater chirps and somewhere in the distance another answers. The splash of sunlight has moved on. The fern is now in shadow, but high up a spider's web has momentarily snared the light. Beads of moisture glisten and sparkle on its tenuous threads. Everywhere the sunlight dances from leaf to leaf. A starling calls, and all is greenness. The air is a sweet perfume of living things. I breathe in, hold its freshness for a moment and breathe out.

THE OUTER REEFS

10

11

12

13

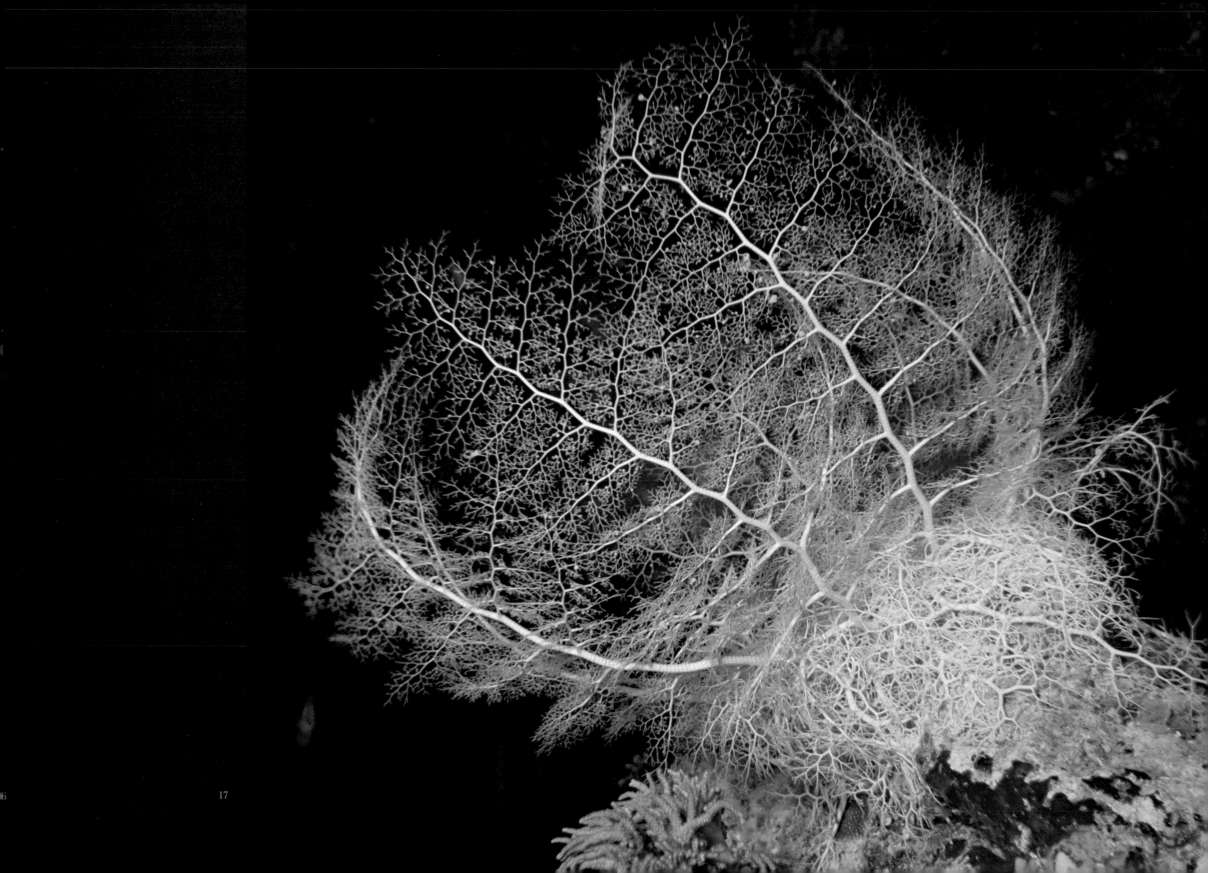

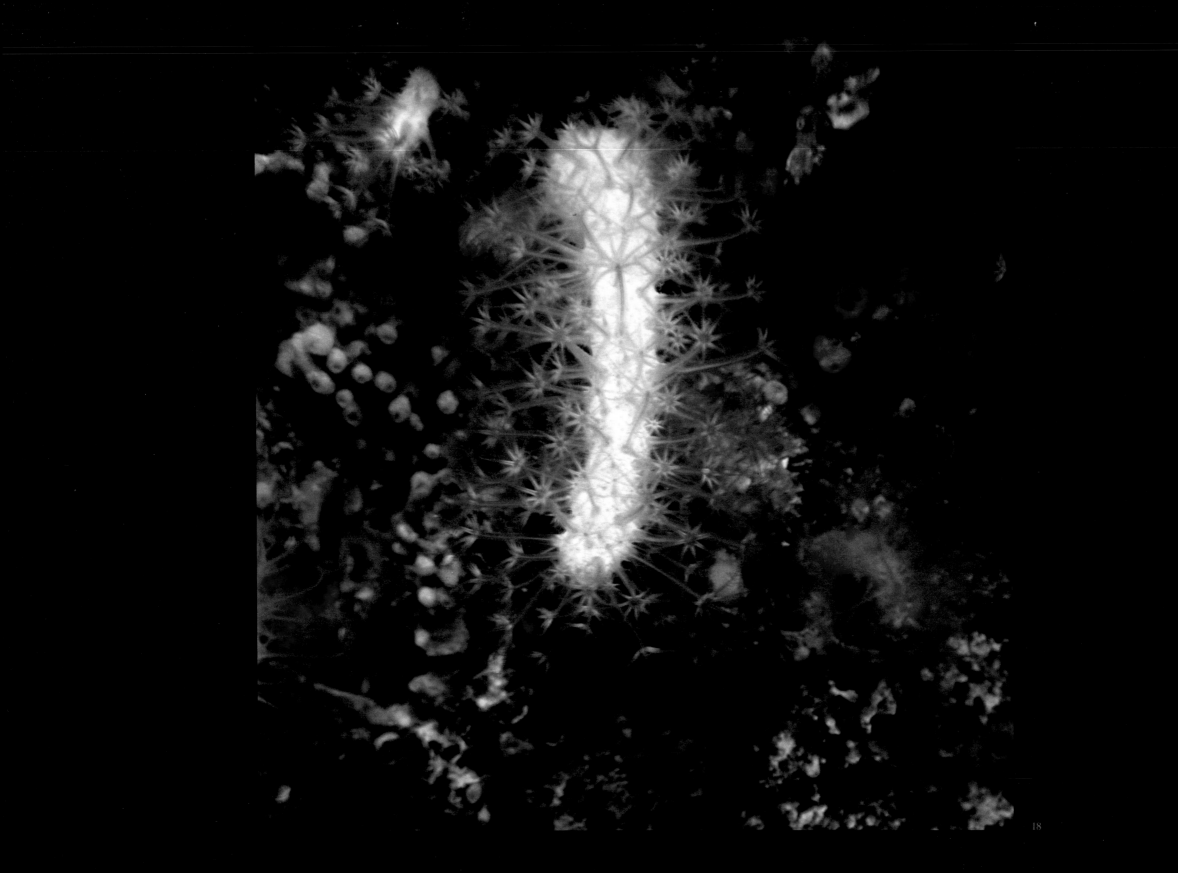

18

22

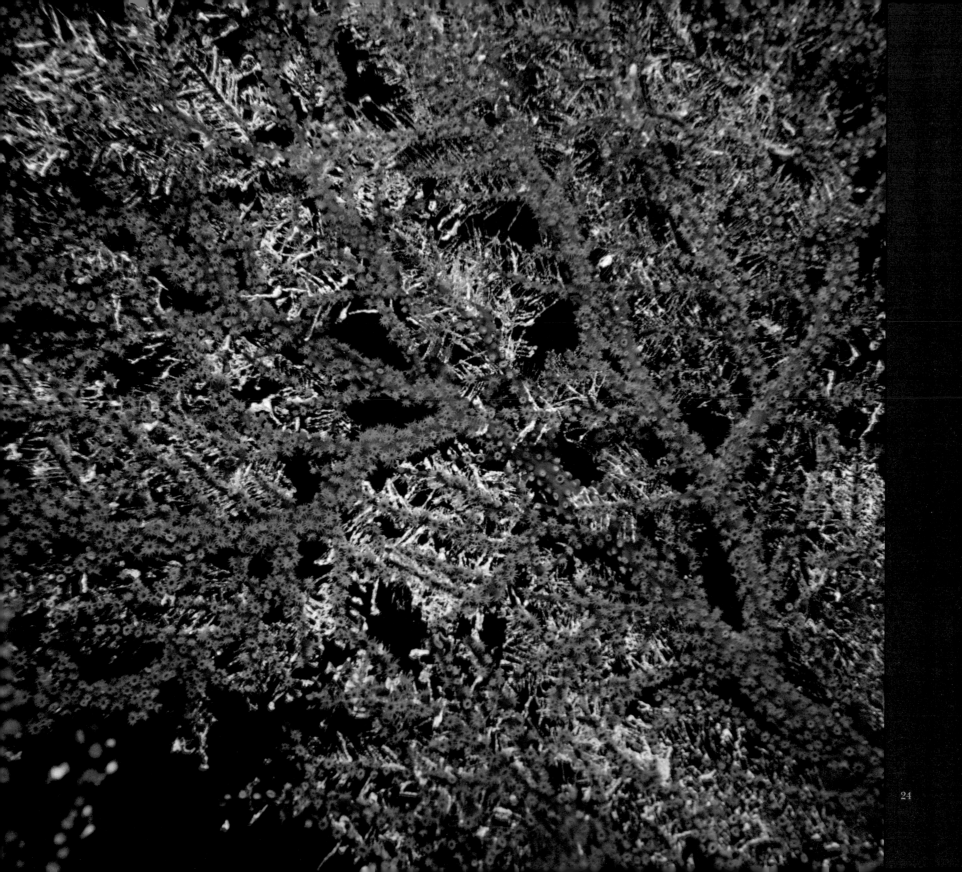

24

32

THE PASSES

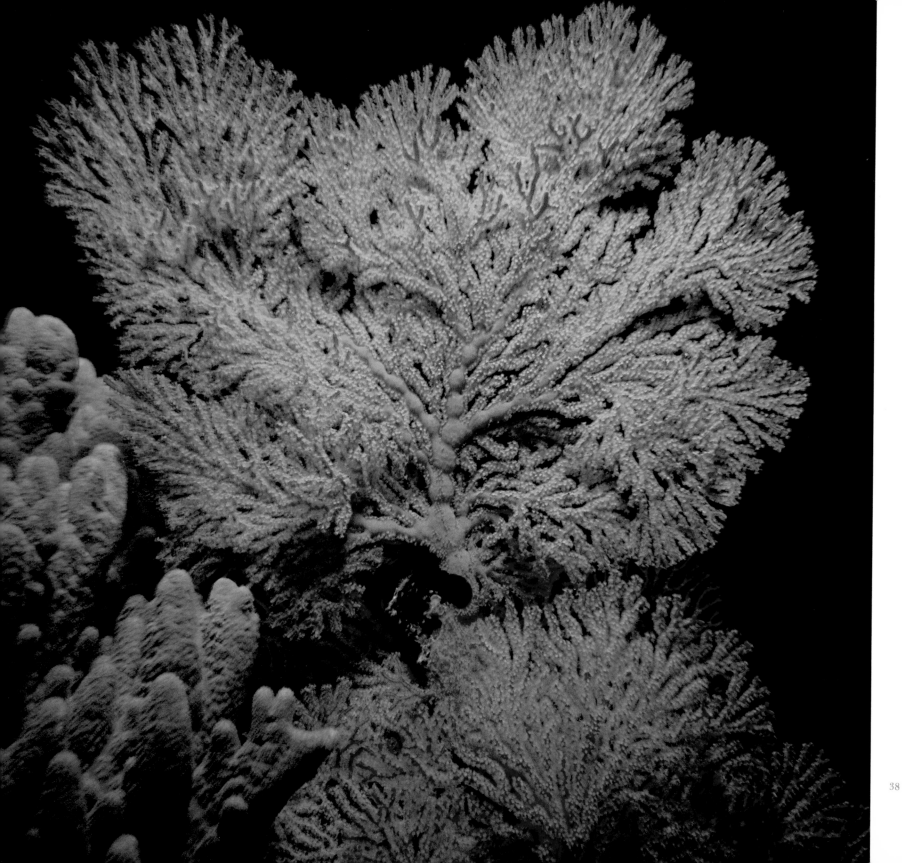

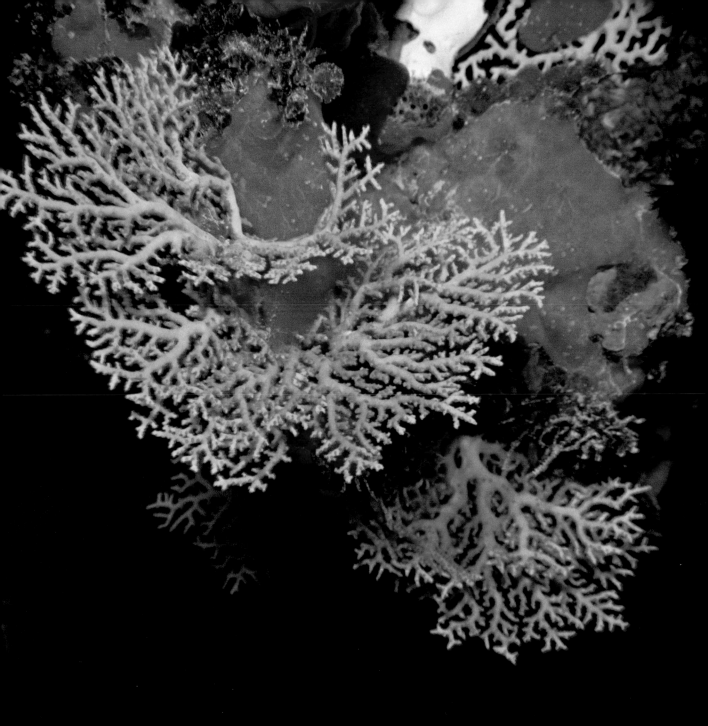

51

THE LAGOONS

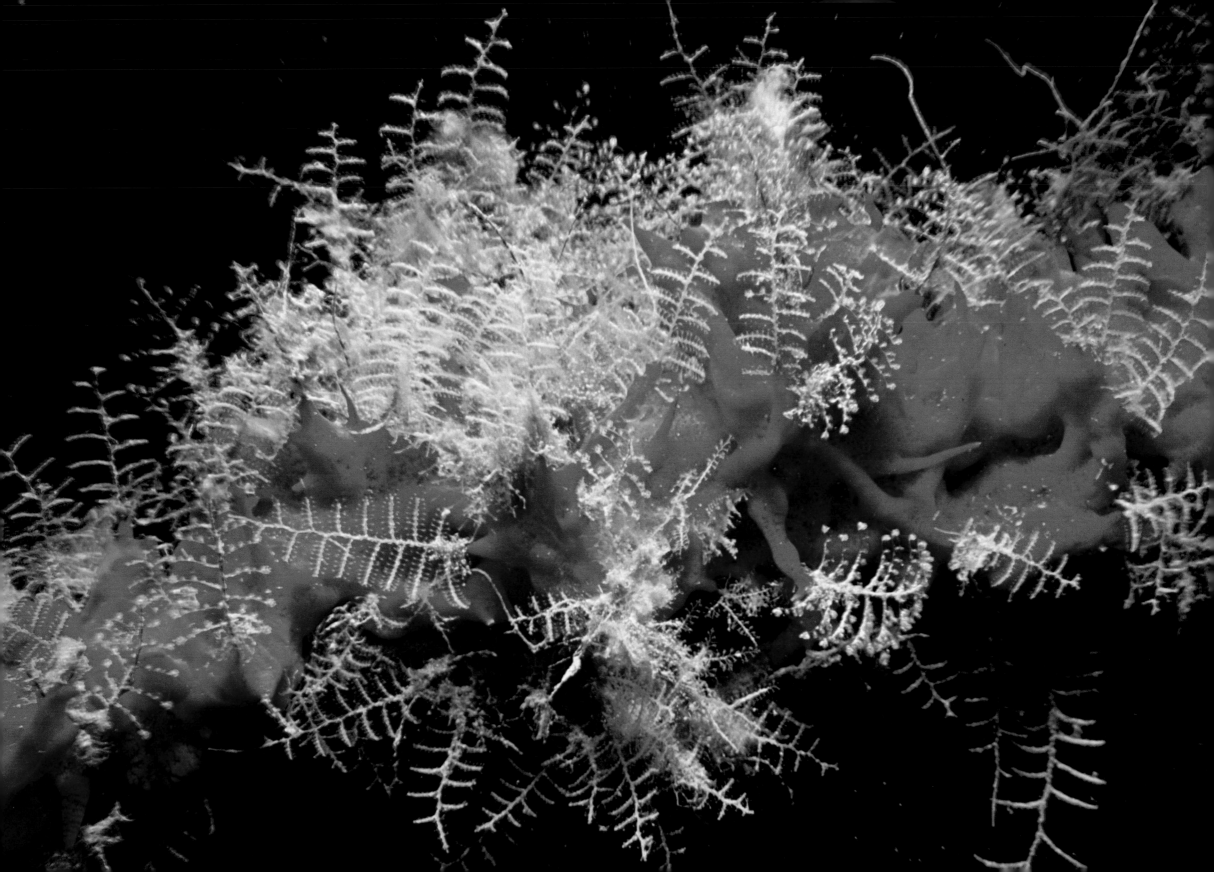

60

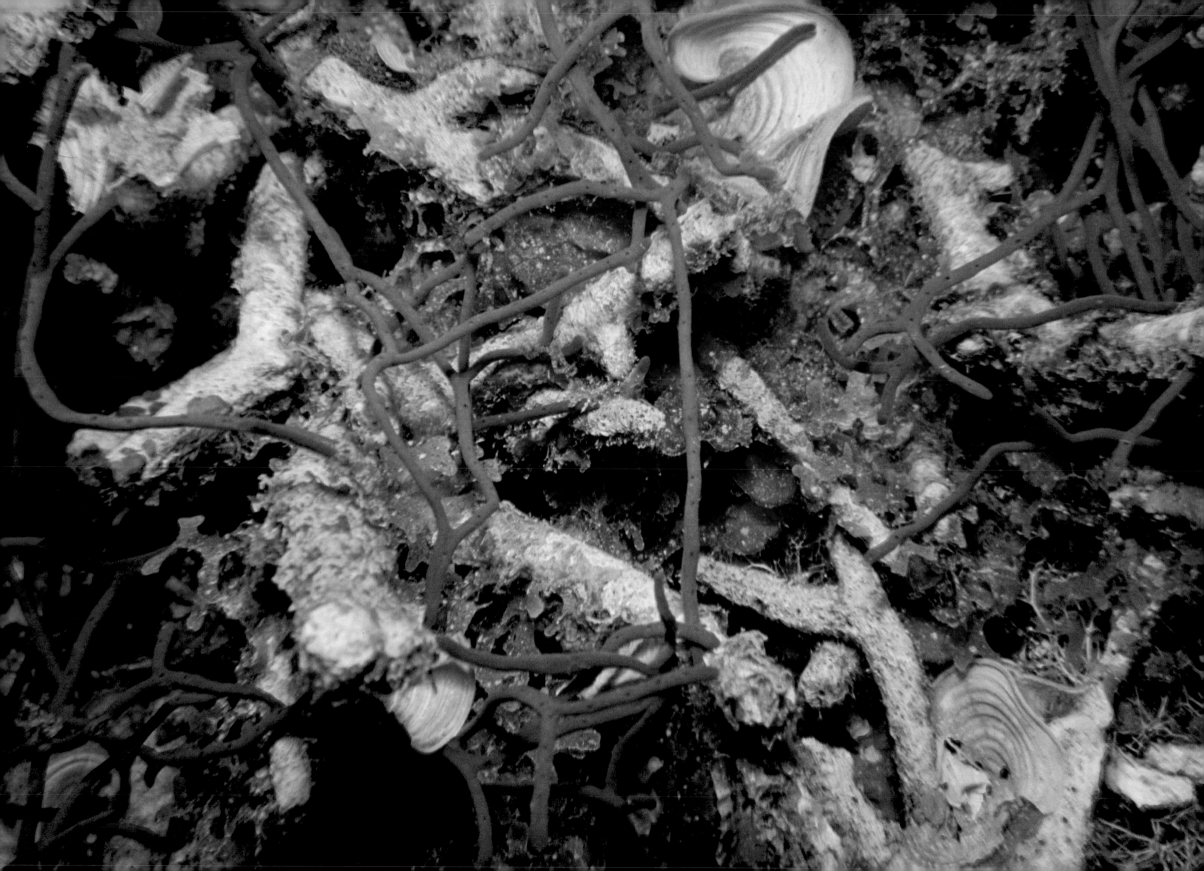

68

69

THE COVES AND MARINE LAKES

93

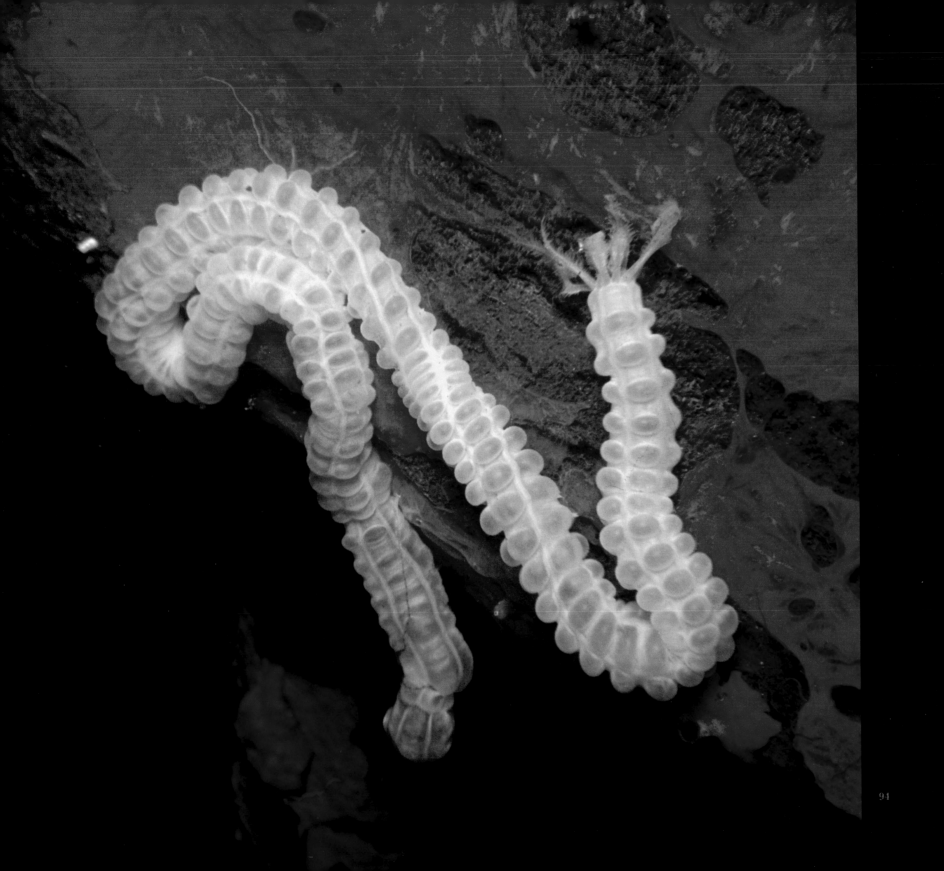

94

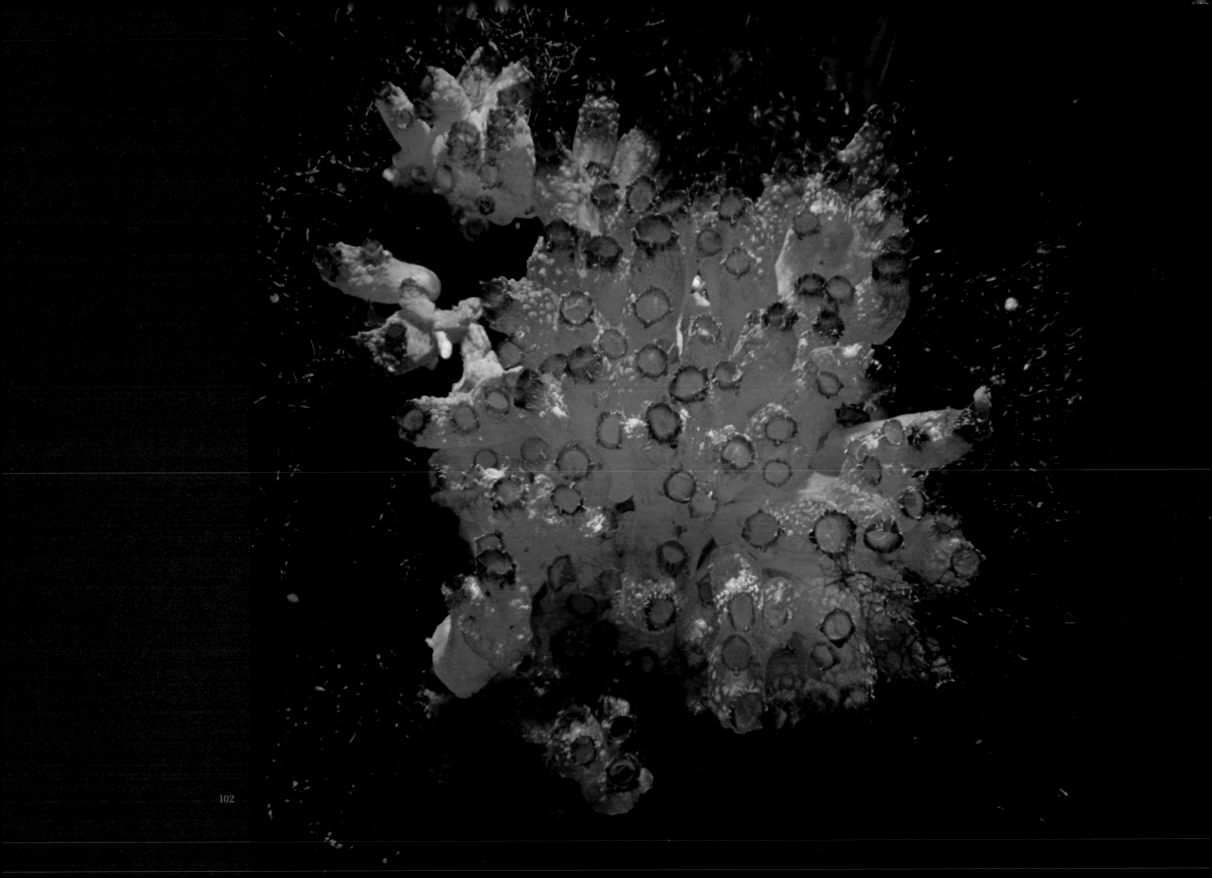

i thank You God for most this amazing
day:for the leaping greenly spirits of trees
and a blue true dream of sky; and for everything
which is natural which is infinite which is yes

(i who have died am alive again today,
and this is the sun's birthday; this is the birth
day of life and of love and wings:and of the gay
great happening illimitably earth)

how should tasting touching hearing seeing
breathing any—lifted from the no
of all nothing—human merely being
doubt unimaginable You?

(now the ears of my ears awake and
now the eyes of my eyes are opened)

COMMENTARY

As moments of beauty, the photographs need no explanation. However, there is much that can be missed when viewing a photograph if one's attention is not drawn to certain aspects of a plant or animal's relationship to its environment. My experience of Belau is only partly revealed in my photography; the text and this commentary give a more complete view.

With the exception of four photographs made during 1973, the 107 plates presented in this book were selected from those made over a five-year period that began October 1967 and ended October 1971. It was during the first of five trips to Belau that I conceived the idea for this book: to take the entire reef complex and separate it into its major areas with the hope that this would enable one to better understand the infinite complexity and beauty of a living environment. My continuing experience during those years determined the book's content and format.

The commentary is in two parts, the first being the practical data. The common names are mostly of my own invention. The scientific names (when known) are given. A question mark after the name means there is still some doubt as the scientific consultant could not always be certain of the identification from looking at my photograph. In some instances, the external characteristics are so similar between one species and another that proper identification of an animal can only be made by examining the teeth, scales on the head, dorsal spines, or by a microscopic examination of spicules.

Furthermore, some of the creatures, such as the Belau cleaner shrimp that is examining the freckled grouper for parasites, are new species. Even though a specimen of the shrimp has been collected and identified, the specific name cannot be published here until it is first officially described in a scientific publication.

The common and scientific names are followed by the approximate size of the subject, the location and approximate depth, and the date the photograph was made. The last part of each commentary contains specific information about the subject and its behavior and importance within the reef environment. Much of this information is from my own observations for which I take final responsibility. The majority of scientists mentioned in the acknowledgments helped primarily in determining the scientific names; the few who read the text and commentary were very helpful in providing facts and in eliminating simple errors. Occasionally a suggestion was made which I did not follow, either because it was contrary to my own experience or to my view of nature. At some point science encounters philosophy and poetry and I have never seen these realms as mutually exclusive. I have tried to avoid errors of fact but whenever possible I have revealed what the facts mean to me. To appreciate facts, we needn't know their ultimate meaning, or if they even have one, but facts never quite explain themselves. They exist but they aren't alive for us unless transmuted through poetry and philosophy as expressions of our encounter with the world that surrounds us. This commentary is, then, an imperfect attempt to make sense of an experience of which I am a part. In it, I have expressed my feelings about the reef's creatures and the need for man to have a more intimate understanding of and appreciation for all living things. No one view can be as large as life itself but it is my hope that the reader will come away from this book with the same feeling that grew within me. Life—an effervescence from the stars—contains the deepest mysteries, all our supremely miraculous hopes, songs, dreams. Here we construct and reconstruct our home and our heaven.

1. Belau is a world of sea and sky and sunlight. The reefs and the land are like a mirage, shimmering for a brief geologic moment, seemingly more miracle than life. This aerial view of Ngcheangel islands was my final photograph of Belau, yet it begins this book because this tiny atoll at Belau's northern extreme is of the open sea. Its oval barrier is continually sculptured by the currents and the wind. Along its eastern edge are four islands, the three southernmost of which are visible in this photograph. Orak island is on the far left with Ngerebelas next to it. A stretch of reef separates Ngerebelas from the lower end of Ngeryungs island on the far right. The lovely turquoise color of the lagoon is the result of its white sand bottom and shallow depth, which is twelve to fifteen feet deep at the southern end. Even the deepest areas of the lagoon are only about forty-five to fifty feet because Ngcheangel is a small atoll (two-and-one-half by four-and-one-half miles) with a shallow pass through its western barrier (visible in this photograph). Beyond Ngcheangel's western rim, seven miles to the northwest, the largely submerged oval of Ngeruangel reef is more sea than land. (700 foot altitude; 29 October 1971)

2. Halfbeaks *Hemiramphus dussumieri* (Valenciennes)? • 1/2 life size • Mutremdiu point, Uchelbeluu reef • Six inches • 16 June 1971

Swimming just beneath the mirror-smooth surface of the outer reef, these two half-beaks seem suspended in air with the sunlight and an intense blue sky and white clouds above them. The open ocean water is extremely clear. The halfbeaks, having evolved a coloration that helps to protect them from predators below, dart near the surface feeding on tiny organisms.

3. In this aerial view, the eastern coast of Babeldaob island is seen with Dimes reef in the foreground. This barrier reef runs northward and is broken by Ngedebaet pass. Beyond, the reef system becomes a fringing reef with no lagoon between it and the island. Dimes is a true barrier reef since it is bounded on the east by the crashing waves of the Pacific Ocean, while on the west are the relatively calm waters of the deep lagoon that separates the coral barrier from Babeldaob island. (1000 foot altitude; 15 August 1969)

4. Surgeonfish *Naso hexacanthus* (Bleeker) • Approximate length 18 inches • Mutremdiu point, Uchelbeluu reef • 100 feet • 27 October 1971

Like many midwater fishes including the black-tip shark on the facing page, these surgeonfish are counter-shaded—dark-colored above and light below. Sunlight from above highlights the upper areas of each fish while the lower surfaces are in shadow. The fish's actual body color, in combination with the natural light, creates a uniform color that blends with the water. In this way the school is a little less conspicuous to its predators. The camouflage effect is not apparent in this photograph because artificial light was used to record the image on film, with the result that the counter-shading is momentarily revealed.

5. Black-tip Shark *Carcharhinus limbatus* (Valenciennes) • Remora *Echeneis naucrates* Linnaeus • Approximate length six feet • Southwest Wall, Ngcheangel islands • 80 feet • 6 September 1971

Like the surgeonfish that live along the wall of the reef, this black-tip shark is also counter-shaded. Its nearly white ventral surface attests to the deep shadow cast by its body. Although sharks have few predators, they still must blend with their surroundings in order to approach their prey. However, any characteristic is always a combination of factors that enables the animal to survive. Even the remora attached to the under surface of the shark is counter-shaded to blend better with its environment which, of course, includes the shark.

Most of the sharks along the outer reef maintain territories. I have returned to the same area of a reef on different occasions and encountered the same sharks. However, once established as a frequent non-competing visitor the sharks lost interest in me. It is always during the first encounter that they are most aggressive, perhaps as a territorial test.

Sharks seem unpredictable to many divers, probably because they are one of the few animals in the sea that men consider really dangerous. A diver must relate to a shark, and if he finds a shark "unpredictable" it is because he notices individual differences of behavior from one encounter to the next. But if, at the same time, the diver noted other factors such as species, size, numbers, location, depth, tide, and water clarity, and kept accurate records over a sufficient period of time, a general pattern would emerge. However, once general behavior is determined, there is still that realm of individuality perhaps more easily conveyed by the word "friendship."

6. Here, photographed from an altitude of 800 feet, is an area of the southwestern barrier reef. On top of the reef in the foreground are the Ngemelis islands, made up of Masch island on the left, Cheleu island and Bailechesengel island on the right. To the left, the barrier stretches away to the north, while in the center of the photograph are the Ngerukuid islands (near distance) and behind them Ulong island. On the horizon to the right is Ngeruktabel island and in the far right distance are the Omekang islands.

This photograph was made during low tide and many sand flats and sand bars are visible along the reef. In the foreground the outer barrier drops off precipitously into very deep water. Due to the particular formation of this reef and its relatively sheltered location, especially along the east side of Bailechesengel island, the marine life luxuriates more than in any other single area of Belau. The reef top is awash at low tide and beginning at the surface the sheer cliff drops away to a depth of 800 feet. All along its face, down to a depth of several hundred feet, a metropolis of encrusting life flourishes. (15 October 1971)

7. Spotted Eagle *Ray Aetobatus narinari* (Euphrasen) • Approximate span five feet • Southwest Wall, Cantin reef, Ngeaur island • 40 feet • 20 October 1971

The outer reefs are home for many ocean creatures including this eagle ray found world wide in tropical waters. Broad distribution attests to its ability to traverse great expanses of open ocean, but this fish frequents the reef environment because it feeds primarily on molluscs bulldozed from the sand.
    At Ngeaur island, shallow reefs are almost non-existent. The few extensions of reef from the land are almost devoid of coral growth down to twenty and thirty feet below the surface. The wave action prevents much life from taking hold, but life becomes more profuse where the reef top curves and drops off into deep water. Here the sturdier corals cover the face of the wall; masses of fishes dart among their branches and hover along the edge of the drop-off.

8. Luna Fusiliers *Caesio lunaris* Cuvier • 1/3 life size • West Wall, Black Beach, Ngeaur island • 55 feet • 19 October 1971

While some fishes are strictly oceanic, there are those that most often make their home along the edge of the outer reefs. These schooling fusiliers feed on planktonic organisms, many of which are the larval young of reef creatures. Since the reef surface is limited, some fishes have adapted to live in the adjacent open water. Many smaller fishes, including the fusiliers, swim in great schools with hundreds of members. They move up and down and along the reef wall feeding on the concentrations of plankton. The fusiliers are fed upon by larger jacks and tuna which in turn attract sharks.

9. Canary Damselfish *Abudefduf aureus* (Cuvier) • Sponge *Gelliodes callista* de Laubenfels • Black Coral *Antipathes arborea* Dana • 1-1/3 times life size • Breu reef, Ngercheu island • 50 feet • 19 May 1971

While many larger fishes frequent the open waters adjacent to the outer reef, this tiny

damselfish makes its home in the nooks and crannies of the wall. The dimly lit caves are relatively safe and provide an abundance of food. Delicate corals and many sponges, such as the salmon-colored one behind the damselfish, attach themselves to the wall and filter tiny organisms from the water currents.

10. Pink Tube Corals *Dendrophyllia gracilis* Milne Edwards & Haime • Lavender Lace Ascidians *Didemnum nekozita* Tokioka • White Lace Ascidians *Didemnum candidum* Savigny • Sponges, Bryozoans, and Algae • 1-1/3 times life size • The Great Reef, Bailechesengel island, Ngemelis islands • 75 feet • 6 July 1971

The Great Reef is almost unique in its profusion of tube corals that live on the slightly undercut walls of the reef face. These corals usually grow in small groups under ledges and are found not only on the outer reefs and passes but also in the lagoons wherever there is a good current of water. A healthy current combined with periods of upwelling and down currents during heavy tidal flows creates an ideal environment for a profusion of life along The Great Reef. The pink tube corals, the little lavender and white ascidians, and the numerous sponges all feed on plankton.

11. White Lace Ascidians *Didemnum candidum* Savigny • Pink Lace Ascidians *Didemnum nekozita* Tokioka • Plastic Ascidian and Red Encrusting Sponge • 1/2 life size • The Great Reef, Bailechesengel island, Ngemelis islands • 40 feet • 30 August 1973

Varying sections of The Great Reef are generally dominated by certain animals. The sloping undersurfaces from thirty to sixty feet deep are inhabited by many tube corals. Ascidians are often equally abundant here, but their numbers increase on the recessed surfaces where the current is subdued and the tube corals are fewer. Evidently the ascidians are more efficient filter feeders, for they can live in areas of less water movement. It is not quite accurate to say that an environment favors a species. Rather, it is the species that phylogenetically adapts to the conditions of a niche while possibly modifying its surroundings to favor its own needs. An environment can be said to favor a species when a mutation survives and is perpetuated because the organism finds itself in surroundings that are better suited to its changed characteristics. Over many generations these characteristics are established, enabling a species to populate similar niches elsewhere.

12. Pink and Lavender Lace Ascidians *Didemnum nekozita* Tokioka • Green Grape Ascidians *Didemnum ternatanum* (Gottschaldt) • Red Encrusting Sponge • 1/2 life size • The Great Reef, Bailechesengel island, Ngemelis islands • 25 feet • 25 August 1973

A brown sponge lives beneath this "painting" of abstract colors. Though it is encrusted with myriad lace ascidians and other sponges, the host's several excurrent openings are evidence of its existence. The sponge is able to limit the number of new settlers on its external surface because it filters and digests most of the plankton unlucky enough to enter the tiny incurrent openings among the colorful squatters.

13. Peppermint Sea Star *Fromia monilis* Perrier • Lavender Lace Ascidians *Didemnum nekozita* Tokioka • Orange Tube Corals *Dendrophyllia elegans* Van Der Horst • Crustose Coralline Algae and Black Encrusting Sponge • Life size • The Great Reef, Bailechesengel island, Ngemelis islands • 50 feet • 20 October 1971

This diminutive sea star is a common inhabitant of crevices and underledges in the cellars of the reef. Unlike cold water sea stars, many tropical species feed on organisms other than molluscs. I have never seen a sea star in the process of feeding on a bivalve in the tropics during the daytime. But since many echinoderms, including sea stars, are active at night, it is possible that they feed on bivalves when darkness comes. It is also likely that many sea stars feed on encrusting life such as sponges and other tiny organisms living on the face of the reef.

14. Pink and Lavender Lace Ascidians *Didemnum nekozita* Tokioka • Crustose Coralline Algae • Yellow, Orange, and Cream Encrusting Sponges • Twice life size • The Great Reef, Bailechesengel island, Ngemelis islands • 60 feet • 21 May 1971

This section of the wall is like an abstract painting, but the rich mosaic is alive, changing little by little—a kaleidoscopic image revolving in slow motion. Green algae grow outward, a larval pink ascidian settles, a bit of orange sponge increases its living space, and another sponge is displaced. In a year this living work of art will have changed. If it seems permanent, as in this photograph, it is only for a brief moment.

15. Disk Algae *Rhipilia orientalis* A. & E.S. Gepp • White Lace Ascidians *Didemnum candidum* Savigny • Sponges • Twice life size • The Great Reef, Bailechesengel island, Ngemelis islands • 50 feet • 23 August 1969

These individual green algae live in a sophisticated spatial relationship to one another and to the other organisms. Like leaves on a tree, their spacing best captures the available sunlight. Each section is set slightly apart from those around it and therefore is able to absorb a share of the sun's rays necessary for photosynthesis.

16. Blue-faced Angelfish *Euxiphipops xanthometapon* (Bleeker) • Pink Tube Corals

Dendrophyllia gracilis Milne Edwards & Haime • 1/2 life size • The Great Reef, Bailechesengel island, Ngemelis islands • 40 feet • 25 August 1971

When night comes to the reef many fishes sleep. In the darkness I came upon this incredibly beautiful angelfish slumbering in a small cave. The beam from my underwater flashlight disturbed him and he slowly emerged. As he drifted sleepily over the night-feeding tube corals, an even more intense flash of light from my camera recorded his beauty on film.

17. Basket Sea Star *Astroglymma sculptum* (Doderlein)? • 1/3 life size • The Great Reef, Bailechesengel island, Ngemelis islands • 15 feet • 25 August 1971

While many fishes sleep at night, other animals such as crabs, urchins, and sea stars emerge from caves and from under coral heads to feed in the gentle darkness. The basket sea star leaves the safety of its crevice under the coral and crawls to its dark promontory. Here, its fragile net of arms are cast into the night tide to snare the countless tiny creatures of the incoming current.

18. Penis Coral, new genus and species • 1-1/3 times life size • The Great Reef, Bailechesengel island, Ngemelis islands • 15 feet • 6 August 1973

Unlike many soft corals that feed day and night with the flowing tides, this penis coral feeds only between sunset and sunrise. When the sun is above the horizon, the animal is no more than a tiny shriveled protrusion extending from the reef wall. With the return of darkness, the coral is aroused to new life. It expands and its graceful polyps extend out from the central column to await what the night will bring.

19. Dandelion Coral *Nidalia lampas* (Thomson & Mackinnon) • Sponge *Eurospongia lobata* Bergquist • Twice life size • The Great Reef, Bailechesengel island, Ngemelis islands • 40 feet • 9 August 1973

Both the penis and dandelion corals are attached to the outer reef wall. The penis corals are most common on the inward curving walls that are less affected by the strongest currents. The dandelion corals inhabit the more recessed ledges. The long slender polyps of both corals are designed for gentle currents. During the day the dandelion coral is no more than a small knob on the end of a short stalk, but come darkness the knob expands. As each slender polyp emerges to feed, the coral resembles a dandelion seed tuft, but in this instance the tiny tentacles of the coral snare plankton instead of the wind.

20. Van Gogh Fusiliers *Pterocaesio chrysozona* (Cuvier & Valenciennes) • 1/3 life size • Mutremdiu point, Uchelbeluu reef • 50 feet • 28 June 1971

For many fishes adapted to life in the open water, schooling is essential for survival. Fishes that school act as a superorganism with individual members comprising the whole. One hundred or 500 pairs of eyes are more likely to see an approaching predator. Though members are eaten by predators, the larger entity still survives, reproduces with itself, and as an "open group" gains new members from the surrounding environment. While each fish is a unit of the school, it is still a distinct individual and is probably so recognized by its immediate companions. If closely observed, even the pattern of the yellow markings on each fusilier is slightly different. Human beings recognize one another by just such subtle distinctions in combination with other characteristics.

21. Chrome Yellow Sponge *Psammaplysella purpurea* (Carter) • Black Coral *Antipathes* sp. • Red Encrusting Sponge *Microciona eurypa* (de Laubenfels)? • 3/4 life size • The Great Reef, Bailechesengel island, Ngemelis islands • 45 feet • 21 May 1971

This chrome yellow sponge colony, living in a cleft of the reef wall, is an altered image of the schooling fusiliers. The colony began as an individual that settled to the bottom and grew by multiplying itself. Actually, the idea of the "individual" is relative. Even humans are entities composed of many specialized organs working together as a functional whole. Beyond this are numerous external relationships necessary to "individual" survival. "No man is an island" is not merely a social truth; it is a biological one as well. The species or the community takes precedence over its individual members. It matters little if member cells of a sponge seem more locked into the colony than do humans or even schooling fish. What is important is the organism's ability to live in a kind of harmony and to reproduce itself. Ultimately there is no good, better, or best form of life. Each species survives as best it can and the only criterion for success is that it exists through whatever mysterious powers of community life invents.

22. Pink Tube Corals *Dendrophyllia gracilis* Milne Edwards & Haime • Blue Sponge *Adocia turquoisia* de Laubenfels? • Red Fire Sponge *Agelas* sp. • Golden and Pink Lace Ascidians *Didemnum* sp. • Tube Corals, Sponges, and Algae • Life size • The Great Reef, Bailechesengel island, Ngemelis islands • 40 feet • 22 May 1971

Since many colors are altered forty feet below the surface due to the sunlight-filtering properties of the water, it seems strange that some sedentary animals display the harlequin hues seen here in artificial light. In natural light, however, differences between the bright red sponge, the tube corals, and the blue sponge are very subtle. Yet there must be some biological necessity for these differences. Whatever the reason, it is a kind of evolutionary miracle that nature somehow delights in a beauty born of necessity—like the fragrant summer flower that attracts the bee.

23. Pink Tube Corals *Dendrophyllia gracilis* Milne Edwards & Haime • Lavender Lace Ascidians *Didemnum nekozita* Tokioka • Red Encrusting Sponge *Tedania* sp. • Mossy Bryozoan *Celleporaria fusca* (Busk) • Life size • The Great Reef, Bailechesengel island, Ngemelis islands • 60 feet • 22 May 1971

Perhaps only through an artist's eye do these colors assume a special significance beyond their intrinsic meaning. Yet the fabric of life is more intricate, more immense than any one view of it. All that any artist can hope to accomplish is to evoke through his own creation a sense of the élan of life, its contrast of forms and colors, its elements of living and dying, light and darkness. If we find our existence somehow beautiful, we are so much the richer for it.

24. Black Coral *Antipathes myriophylla* Pallas • Zoanthids *Parazoanthus* sp. • Life size • The Great Reef, Bailechesengel island, Ngemelis islands • 40 feet • 6 July 1971

Like the wire corals, this species of black coral is attached to the reef wall. At one time the black coral was living but gradually it was overgrown with tiny zoanthids, anemone-like colonial animals, with each zoanthid joined at its base to those next to it. Although the black coral's flesh has died, its skeleton remains as a support for the mass of zoanthids. A casual observer might think that the zoanthids are the polyps of a living sea fan. However, the tell-tale sign is the accumulation of white sediment on the feathery branches of the black coral. A living black coral or sea fan would not acquire such an accumulation of sediment since its polyps would either consume the particles or reject them.

Zoanthids generally grow on the surfaces of other animals such as shells, sponges, bryozoans, and corals, partly destroying the host in the process. Like many parasites, certain species of zoanthids have adapted to living on specific hosts.

25. Hawksbill Turtle *Eretmochelys imbricata* (Linnaeus) • Chalice Castle Coral *Pachyseris speciosa* (Dana) • 1/2 life size • The Great Reef, Bailechesengel island, Ngemelis islands • 90 feet • 6 July 1971

Hawksbill turtles frequent the passes and even the lagoons but they most often live on the edge of the outer reef. If they are not swimming along the reef, they can sometimes be found sleeping on the bottom, near or under the ledge of a large coral head. Though they must come to the surface to breathe, they can stay underwater for long periods of time when resting. In natural light at a distance, a hawksbill turtle blends well with a coral background because its muted colors and mottled pattern act as a camouflage. Only in a close-up view with artificial light is it possible to capture the animal's rich coloration of rust, yellow, black, and tan.

26. Silver Crinoid *Cenometra bella* Hartlaub • Red Sea Whips *Ellisella andamanensis* (Simpson) • 3/4 life size • Breu reef, Ngercheu island • 75 feet • 19 May 1971

This crinoid (a relative of the sea stars) and the red sea whips are plankton feeders. Both are most active when the tide is either ebbing or flowing. It is during these times that an abundance of plankton passes along the face of the reef. The sea whips, a coral colony, wait until there is a fairly strong current before expanding their polyps to feed. When the current begins to slack somewhat, such as shortly before high tide, the polyps cease feeding and contract. In contrast, the crinoid has a broader surface and is able to trap a fair amount of food before the diminishing current ceases. Eventually the crinoid — like the sea whips — stops feeding and curls up its arms to await the tide's ebb.

27. Freckled Grouper *Epinephelus coatesi* (Whitley) • Belau Cleaner Shrimp *Leandrites* new species • 1-1/4 times life size • Mutremdiu point, Uchelbeluu reef • 45 feet • 30 June 1971

The reef community contains a wealth of interspecies relationships that are not merely predator-prey activities though they are often largely based on predator-prey imperatives. What we term "parasites" cling to life by attaching themselves to the various surfaces of other animals, feeding on the host's tissues. Shrimps live by feeding on organisms smaller than themselves. Fishes, too, must live and will do whatever they can to rid themselves of parasites. By some strange evolutionary alchemy, intricate interrelationships have evolved over the centuries. Today a freckled grouper swims over to a darkened promontory under a ledge where a little shrimp climbs aboard and searches for parasitic copepods. When the shrimp approaches the fish's head, the grouper opens its mouth, signifying that it needs the inside area cleaned. The little shrimp inspects the grouper's lower lip and then disappears inside. The grouper keeps its mouth open and refrains from eating the shrimp. After a brief time, the shrimp

emerges and leaves the body of the grouper. The fish goes on its way but will return often during the day to be "gone over" again. The shrimp will not find and eat all the grouper's parasites, as some will survive and the grouper will gradually acquire new ones. Not every individual fish, shrimp, or parasite survives, but each species endures until a new combination of factors terminates one expression of life. What still remain are varying constellations of relationships. If one imperative of animal life is based upon the consumption of organic matter, then most creatures, including man, are predators if not parasites. Man is both beneficial to and dependent upon a maze of biological relationships. If these relationships seem wholly mechanical or somehow lacking in "spirit," it is because we have yet to gain an appreciation of the miracle of life. If there is any miracle in this universe, it's that all living things exist in endless diversity, even if man in his own struggle for survival labels some "good" and others "evil."

28. Freckled Groupers *Epinephelus coatesi* (Whitley) • Red Gorgonian and Orange Sponge • 4/5 life size • Mutremdiu point, Uchelbeluu reef • 45 feet • 2 July 1971

Sometimes it can be risky to include colors as part of the names of marine animals since, like chameleons or octopuses, many creatures can change their colors in a moment of time. These two freckled groupers are the same species as the one being cleaned but because they are against a light-colored bottom with a splash of orange sponge, they have altered their color accordingly. During several weeks of intensive photographic activity, I managed to become acquainted with three groupers living in this cave area. Each one became accustomed to having its picture taken, usually alone. Obviously they didn't know quite what was happening but the periodic flash of light must have intrigued them for they would occasionally vie for my attention, as they did when this photograph was made. The three groupers were not all the same size and there was a ranking system. One day when I was trying to photograph the grouper on the right, the one on the left swam forward and upstaged my model. Was it jealousy...curiosity...or just wanting to be included in the experience?

29. Lizardfish *Synodus variegatus* (Lacépède) • Staghorn Corals *Acropora surculosa* (Dana)? • 1-1/3 times life size • Mutremdiu point, Uchelbeluu reef • 20 feet • 16 June 1971

Like two camouflaged surface-to-air missiles, these lizardfish are resting on a platform of dead staghorn coral encrusted with algae. Their color blends beautifully into the coral background. When a school of small fish swims overhead, a lizardfish readies itself by tilting its head further upward. At just the right moment the predator launches with lightning speed. The school scatters but the lizardfish has snared its prey, and quickly returns to the bottom while swallowing its meal. The lizardfish often misses its mark and must try again and again.

Behind these lizardfish is a living colony of staghorn coral. The formation is more truncated than many species that live in the quieter waters of the lagoons. On certain areas of the outer reef top, where the surge is greatest, corals are even more truncated at depths of thirty to forty feet than this specimen which is growing on a fairly protected reef top. In Belau there are approximately fifty different species of staghorn corals. Some grow only on the outer reef front and reef flat while others grow in the passes or in very quiet waters deep in the lagoon. Many species may live in several different habitats, but at the extremes of the overall environment differing characteristics usually exist.

30. Rock Flathead *Platycephalus beauforti* Knapp • Staghorn Coral Skeletons *Acropora* sp. • Green Grape Ascidians *Didemnum ternatanum* (Gottschaldt) • Algae • 1-1/3 times life size • Mutremdiu point, Uchelbeluu reef • 25 feet • 6 June 1971

On the reef top there are areas of dead coral debris between formations of living coral. Since there is hardly an area in the sea that is not inhabited by some form of life, it is not surprising that the dead coral bottom is occupied by this rock flathead. Through the process of evolutionary adaptation, the fish has come to resemble its environment. Even its eyes are camouflaged. Looking more like an alligator than a fish, the flathead rests motionless on the bottom, usually under a coral overhang. Here it waits for hours, perhaps not "with gently smiling jaws" but just as patiently for some unsuspecting fish to pass.

31. Bronze Spot Sea Cucumber *Bohadschia argus* Jaeger • Staghorn Coral *Acropora surculosa* (Dana)? • Calcareous Green Algae *Halimeda* sp. • Green Grape Ascidians *Didemnum ternatanum* (Gottschaldt) • 2/3 life size • Mutremdiu point, Uchelbeluu reef • 25 feet • 10 August 1971

One night, while swimming over the reef top, I came across this sea cucumber acting like a cobra. Once before I had seen another species of sea cucumber rear up into the current and release a milky substance which the current carried away. Possibly the sea cucumber was releasing spermatozoa into the water. However, when one happens upon such an odd-looking creature at night it is easy to lapse into an anthropomorphic frame of mind and imagine that there is always the one in a trillion chance this sea cucumber is conversing with the stars.

32. Lightning Butterflyfish *Chaetodon punctatofaciatus* Cuvier • False Finger Coral *Stylophora mordax* (Dana) • Staghorn Corals *Acropora* sp. • Life size • Mutremdiu point, Uchelbeluu reef • 20 feet • 15 June 1971

This little butterflyfish is less exotic-looking than many of the Indo-Pacific butterflyfishes. However, in each species there always seems to be a natural balance of color and pattern that evokes a wholly pleasing effect so that nature is lovely even in its most modest garb. Butterflyfishes are common on the outer reef, seen most often on the top and at its seaward edge where the reef begins its downward curve to the depths. In these areas there is the largest concentration of stony coral formations, such as the false finger coral (right foreground) and the various species of staghorn coral. These dainty eaters feed on coral polyps and the corals serve as hideaways in times of danger or as objects to sleep under at night.

33. Taken at an altitude of 600 feet, this photograph shows Ngerchelong peninsula, the northern end of Babeldaob island, in the distance. In the foreground is Ngebard reef, an extension of the western barrier reef system. The land of which it was once a part has submerged and what remains is a network of coral-formed structures adjacent to the Philippine Sea. The pass, Tochelel Ngebard, winds through the reef like a river system connecting the lagoon with the open ocean and facilitating the flow of tidal waters through the reef. (29 October 1971)

34. Long-snouted Hawkfish *Oxycirrhites typus* Bleeker • Black Coral *Antipathes myriophylla* Pallas • Twice life size • Ngerutechetachel reef, Towachelmlengui pass, Babeldaob island • 35 feet • 26 August 1969

The sides of a pass are bounded by the reef, a living river bank. Its walls are alive with many of the same encrusting organisms found on the outer reef. Perched on the branches of a black coral tree, a tiny hawkfish watches the world go by. This charming little fish ranges over an area of several yards, swimming from coral to ledge and back. By the shape of his mouth, it is obvious he is a dangerous creature. If, as humans, we smile, it is because we are not tiny shrimp or crab larvae. Then we would hide in a crevice lest the silver-eyed, candy-cane giant see us and inhale us down his slurp-gun mouth, helpless specks sucked in by the vacuum action of his terrifying jaws.

35. Boring Sea Urchins *Echinostrephus aciculatus* Agassiz • Pink Encrusting Sponge *Spirastrella* sp. • Rust Algae and Coral • 1-1/3 times life size • Ngerutechetachel reef, Towachelmlengui pass, Babeldaob island • 40 feet • 21 August 1969

While many animals and plants build up the reef, others tend to break it down by boring into it. Bivalves and spiral plume worms are borers, along with these tiny brown sea urchins. The urchins begin their excavation work as juveniles and as they grow, they fashion a home in the coral. Scientists are not certain of the exact method by which the excavation is accomplished. It could be that the urchins excrete a solvent that eats away the limestone or use their spines to abrade the surface or perhaps they use a combination of both. If their spines wear away it matters little since they continue to grow, whereas the limestone substrate is slowly hollowed out. The urchins are relatively safe from attack in their snug little holes with only a cluster of spines protruding from the face of the reef. During daylight hours they rest. At night, under cover of darkness, the urchins emerge to feed on algae and other organic matter.

36. Ulong island is seen here in the near distance with its quarter-mile stretch of white sand beach. In the foreground, just below the surface of the water, is an old coral formation atop the barrier reef which borders Ngerumekaol pass. Only a few hardy corals cling to the top of this old coral structure. On calm days the ocean seems placid but during storms many shallow reef corals are destroyed. Consequently, the zone richest in life begins deeper down the sides of the pass.

The greatest depth of the pass is fifty feet but at its mouth it is only about thirty-five feet deep due to increased coral growth across the bottom. Here, the current is less constricted and moves more slowly. (24 August 1971)

37. Picasso Butterflyfish *Chaetodon meyeri* Bloch & Schneider • Mountain Coral *Porites lutea* Milne Edwards & Haime • Life size • Ngerumekaol pass, Ulong island • 40 feet • 20 August 1969

The existence of nearly 200 species of butterflyfishes seems somehow less amazing than the fact that their colors and patterns so easily distinguish them from one another. Only a few of the species closely resemble one another in appearance, possibly confusing the casual observer. The Picasso is one of the most striking members of the butterflyfish family and could hardly be confused with another species. In some ways, however, its body markings resemble *Chaetodon ornatissimus*. The same basic background color of white, black, and yellow exists, but in contrast to the Picasso butterflyfish, *C. ornatissimus* has bright orange center stripes that are diagonal but end in straight lines instead of curving up at the ends. This single combination of orange color and its slightly altered pattern make the species easily distinguishable.

What has evolved is a living "national flag." Some markings of the flag are determined by such factors as the need to camouflage the eyes. To confuse would-be predators,

many butterflyfishes have a bar running through the eye and some have a false-eye spot near the tail. However, predators are, or with practice become, more discerning and therefore such markings aid survival but do not ensure it.

Another factor that contributes to this biological "flag" is the fish's relationship to the water medium which determines its shape and confines the color pattern within it. The water also acts as a filter; since red is lost very quickly it rarely exists in butterflyfishes that depend on their own and other fishes' ability to see colors. Orange is still seen as orange down to 150 feet and yellow is still visible at 300 feet. Therefore, such colors are common in butterflyfishes that usually live in depths down to fifty or 100 feet but rarely deeper than 150 feet. If red usually goes black at sixty feet, the markings of the fish might as well be black, which is the case.

Last, but far from least, the artistry of the flag is determined by inter-species as well as intra-species identification. Most obvious is the need for each fish to identify its own species for pairing and reproduction. Most butterflyfishes do pair and live together beyond the periodic reproductive relationship. They also maintain territories, and if the territorial flag is part of their person others of their own species will see it and most often avoid intrusion or violent confrontation. This is not only true for members of the same species but applies to different species that may be direct competitors. Consequently, a natural spacing occurs which minimizes conflicts. There is always competition and the young and healthy replace the old and ailing. However, somewhere there is that middle ground where the flag prevails, making life a little less "red in tooth and cláw," more bearable or, biologically speaking, more ecologically balanced.

38. Orange Sea Fan *Melithea squamata* (Nutting) • Leather Coral *Cladiella* sp. • Life size • Ngerumekaol pass, Ulong island • 30 feet • 13 August 1971

No doubt diversity is one of the essentials of life throughout the entire universe. It certainly is true on Earth where, in the sea, marine animals have evolved through diversity of behavior which affects, among other things, their feeding habits. A sea fan hardly resembles a butterflyfish—an advantage to both creatures. The sea fan may feed on drifting fish eggs, but the fish produces enough eggs to perpetuate the species despite such losses. In turn, the butterflyfish may occasionally feed on the polyps of the sea fan along with many other organisms in its immediate area. The individual coral polyps die but the colony continues to live as do the butterflyfishes. These two ways of life enable these different animals to coexist within the same environment with a minimum of direct competition and conflict. The value of diversity is further illustrated when we see that most animals including butterflyfishes maintain territories for the express purpose of keeping members of their own species at a comfortable distance. Territory is the equivalent of space. If all organisms required a great amount of space between themselves and all others, life would not be as we know it, infinitely complex and varied.

39. Bigeye *Priacanthus hamrur* Forskål • Life size • Ngerumekaol pass, Ulong island • 30 feet • 25 October 1967

Shallow water diurnal fishes are seldom red, but deep water and nocturnal fishes are often this color. Although this bigeye was photographed at midday in open shallow water, its presence there is rare. Bigeyes are usually nocturnal and feed primarily at night when their red color could appear dark brown or black. However, a bigeye is also capable of changing its color to reddish blotches on a paler background. This ability to change color is accomplished by simultaneously expanding and contracting various pigment aggregates of chromatophore cells in the skin. As in a Seurat painting, the colors are blended by the eye of the beholder into another color or combination of markings. Many fishes use this color-change to blend in with their background. At night, sleeping fishes often change to a mottled body pattern to elude nocturnal predators, but the bigeye has large eyes that enable it to hunt by starlight or even on cloudy nights that to us would seem pitch black.

40. Sun and Stars Angelfish *Euxiphipops navarchus* (Cuvier & Valenciennes) • False Finger Coral *Stylophora mordax* (Dana) • Life size • Ngerumekaol pass, Ulong island • 20 feet • 13 August 1971

The sun and stars angelfish is quite rare in Belauan waters. Essentially an outer reef inhabitant, it also lives in the passes and like most of the small-mouthed reef fishes, grazes upon coral polyps, algae, tiny crustaceans, and sponges. Although this angelfish has a very conspicuous "national flag" or "poster marking," it is also obvious that the fish's eye is masked as a means of protection. The orange and blue pattern is similar at both ends of the animal, which no doubt helps to confuse a predator.

One fascinating feature, particularly of the larger angelfishes, is the incredible color-pattern transformation that takes place as the juveniles grow into adulthood. The juvenile sun and stars angelfish is very similar to the adult but there are other inhabitants of the passes such as the emperor angelfish *Pomacanthus imperator* that change dramatically as they mature. The base color of a juvenile emperor angelfish is dark blue with a pattern of brilliant white circular markings on it. As this fish grows, the white circular lines alter to a more convoluted pattern. With continued growth they fade and yellow lines appear. The base color also changes from its original deep blue to turquoise and the yellow lines run more diagonally to the head where black and yellow markings are accented with neon-blue borders. When looking at the juveniles, one would never guess their relationship to the adults, just as one would never imagine the caterpillar's relationship to a butterfly without first observing, step by step, its metamorphosis.

When I asked myself how this contrast in body markings might aid survival, I remembered the territorial significance of many of these markings as national flags. Essentially, the flag, as a biological aid, minimizes territorial intrusion by other members of the same species. Up to a degree, "no trespassing" aids survival, but beyond a certain level of repulsion the flag may have adverse effects on pairing, reproduction, and on the more economical sharing of living space.

The differences between some juvenile and adult markings may be an excellent illustration of how diversity arises of necessity through the evolutionary process. In an environment of limited space and food, an adult emperor angelfish can abide the presence of a juvenile because it does not wear the same flag. In this way, the young are secure in an adult world and thus the species is better able to survive. This theory is reinforced when we realize that certain juvenile fishes, including some angelfishes, are cleaners. During their youth, they pick and eat parasites from larger fishes. Their distinct juvenile markings advertise them as cleaners and enable them to live within close proximity to their own adult species with little or no conflict due to their temporary, non-competitive roles.

41. Thorny Oyster *Spondylus aurantius* Lamarck? • White Lace Coral *Stylaster sanguineus* Milne Edwards & Haime • Disk Algae *Rhipilia orientalis* A. & E.S. Gepp • Red Encrusting Sponge *Microciona eurypa* (de Laubenfels)? • Crustose Coralline Algae • Life size • Ulach pass, Ngcheangel islands • 45 feet • 1 September 1971

Thorny oysters occasionally live under ledges in the lagoon and even in some of the interior marine lakes, but they thrive in greatest abundance on the outer reef fronts and in the passes where the open ocean currents provide an abundance of food. The thorny oyster is actually a scallop which attaches itself to the wall, where its shell provides an additional surface for other sedentary animals and plants. In this strange and fascinating undersea world, it is obvious that no organism lives in isolation.

Like all scallops, thorny oysters have a row of tiny eyes along each edge of their two shells. The eyes are extremely sensitive to changes in light intensity. The shadow from an approaching predator can alert them to danger. However, from my own experience

I have found these bivalves to be even more sensitive to slight displacements of water. Even if approached very slowly, they often detect my prescence and shut their shells tightly. No doubt the combined change in light intensity and water pressure serves to warn them. At night, a thorny oyster opens its shell wider to feed on plankton and seems much less bothered by sudden light or pressure changes. Perhaps its biological clock is not programmed to fear predators at night since those who would normally prey upon the scallop are probably daytime feeders such as fishes. Consequently, even the extreme change from darkness to the direct beam of an underwater flashlight does not alarm it enough to make it close its shell.

42. Leopard Shark *Stegostoma tigrinum* Bonnaterre • Approximate length six feet • Ulach pass, Ngcheangel islands • 95 feet • 2 August 1971

Certain oceanic sharks apparently never stop swimming since to do so would drastically decrease the water flow over their gills, causing them to suffocate from lack of oxygen and a build-up of carbon dioxide in their systems. On the other hand, there are less active varieties such as nurse sharks and this leopard shark seen resting on the deep sandy bottom of Ulach pass. The water is exceedingly clear on an incoming tide. The shark faces into the flow of the current which provides the necessary exchange of gases. The shark occasionally yawns, which probably helps to flush its gills.

As is apparent from this photograph, not all sharks are ferocious "man eaters." Although I encounter sharks quite often in my diving activities, I still can't understand what seems to me to be man's paranoid attitude toward them. I am certain that men have killed more sharks than the other way around and yet, when diving, I've never sensed a conspiracy on the part of sharks to eliminate man from the face of the earth in anywhere near the overzealous manner by which humans go about destroying those who might harm them. No doubt this is the reason why I see a less ferocious, more personal image; one that is lyrical...always an affirmation of life.

43. Pink Lace Coral *Stylaster sanguineus* Milne Edwards & Haime • Disk Algae *Rhipilia orientalis* A. & E.S. Gepp • Red Encrusting Sponge *Microciona eurypa* (de Laubenfels)? • 1-1/2 times life size • Ulach pass, Ngcheangel islands • 45 feet • 4 August 1971

Large coral structures form the walls of the pass. Very often these walls are deeply undercut in various places with overhanging ceilings that seem to be the special domain of lace corals, particularly when the ceilings are adjacent to the tidal currents

flowing beneath them. The corals that grow there expose their broad surface to the current in the same manner that sea fans do to facilitate feeding. Unlike most stony corals, this lace coral's color is incorporated in its skeleton and does not fade when the polyps die.

Although algae need sunlight to carry on photosynthesis, it is obvious that some marine plants are adapted to living under ledges where there is much less light than on the reef top. Occasionally scientists, but more often popular writers, give the impression that there is some ideal environment for life and that the deeps or other areas are lesser places to live. The truth is that life flourishes in the most unlikely places. If men have their limits of comfort and comprehension, it is precisely because they are men. Other creatures may also have certain limits that might preclude the development of atomic reactors and symbolic thought, but in the world to which they have adapted they nevertheless exist quite well.

44. White Tube Corals *Dendrophyllia gracilis* Milne Edwards & Haime • Grape Algae *Caulerpa racemosa* (Forskål) • White Lace Ascidians *Didemnum candidum* Savigny • 1-1/4 times life size • Ulach pass, Ngcheangel islands • 70 feet • 4 September 1971

Of the many kinds of Indo-Pacific corals, this particular type of tube coral probably feeds exclusively at night. The photographs of the tube corals in The Outer Reefs section of the book were taken during daylight hours and therefore have contracted tentacles, but after the sun sets and dusk comes to the undersea world, these tube corals expand in order to feed. Each coral traps plankton with its tentacles and then inserts each tentacle into its red-rimmed mouth cavity where the food is removed and digested.

45. Bumphead Parrotfish *Bolbometopon muricatus* (Cuvier & Valenciennes) • Calcareous Green Algae *Halimeda incrassata* (Ellis) Lamouroux • 1/3 life size • Ulach pass, Ngcheangel islands • 45 feet • 9 September 1971

The many different species of parrotfish have a variety of sleeping habits. Some parrotfish sleep on the dead coral rubble of the bottom at night and change to mottled coloration. Others seek out small caves in the coral base and surround themselves with a mucous membrane which acts as a protective cocoon. Though it most often travels with a school during the daylight hours, the bumphead parrotfish sleeps alone at night. During full moon, the bumphead seeks the darkness of deeper water. It sometimes sleeps near the reef wall in the shallower waters of Ulach pass when the night sky is filled only with stars.

In the darkness, the beam from the flashlight held by my Belauan diving companion blinded the animal. The creature was helpless against our rude invasion. In the harsh light surrounded by darkness, the bumphead's fused teeth and pterodactyl-like forehead made me feel like a participant in an age long before the emergence of man. As I photographed, I tried to imagine how many millions of years of evolution went into creating this organism of fin, eye, and flesh. I continued to photograph until the film was finished. Since it was our last dive of the night, my companion handed me the flashlights and took my diving knife. He had decided to obtain tomorrow's meal. I watched with rising apprehension as he approached the parrotfish and stabbed it through the middle. With one thrust the animal was pinned to the coral wall. It twisted, struggled, and then with one violent lunge freed itself and swam upward into the darkness. I picked it up in the flashlight beam and followed it until the dark waters consumed the wounded animal. My diving companion motioned excitedly for me to follow the dying creature. I hesitated, not feeling the spirit of the hunt. As a photographer I had accomplished my hunting with my camera and by some mysterious alchemy the predator-prey relationship was transmuted to something new. This once-sleeping fish had become a friend. Mechanically, I continued to shine the light toward the open water where suddenly, swimming into the beam, came the fish returning like a burning fighter plane in a midnight blitz, trailing a streak of blazing red blood. It descended crazily, seeking the light of a false sun while I watched all the stars of its tiny briefest universe whirl into darkness.

46. Green Tube Coral *Tubastraea micrantha* (Ehrenberg) • 1-1/3 times life size • Ulach pass, Ngcheangel islands • 60 feet • 7 August 1971

This large colony of green tube corals feeds primarily at night when plankton is more abundant. However, during strong monthly tidal flows, the polyps will also feed during daylight hours when the stronger currents create a concentration of organic matter in the water. This abundance of food evidently triggers the polyps' feeding mechanism. However, they make one concession to their nocturnal habit; they don't expand their polyps fully during the daytime. Many fishes feed on coral polyps, so if they are not fully expanded there is less chance they will be eaten. These large coral polyps are much safer feeding at night when many coral-eating fishes are asleep.

This photograph shows the exquisite beauty of these night-blooming creatures, but there is one experience only words can describe since the science of photography still lacks the capabilities of the human eye and mind. This photograph illustrates the beauty of the lighted subject, but when the underwater flashlights are extinguished one's eyes will presently discern a twinkling of stars. The tiny silver flashes are the planktonic organisms drifting against the coral's tentacles, tumbling from one to the next as shimmering points of bioluminescence. The unseen presence of the coral colony is sensed only as a silhouette in the darkness.

47. Fan Crinoid *Comanthus parvicirra* (J. Muller) • Porous Coral *Porites iwayamaensis* Eguchi • Calcareous Green Algae *Halimeda* sp. • Life size • Ulach pass, Ngcheangel islands • 35 feet • 7 August 1971

Many crinoids, including those that live on the gorgonians, are capable of moving elsewhere but they feed day and night, rarely changing their position from one year to the next. On the other hand, there are some crinoids that exercise their ability to move and feed mainly at night. During the day these crinoids, like the basket sea stars, secret themselves under a coral head. They remain there until the last golden rays of the sun darken above the horizon; then, they emerge from their hiding places and climb to the top of a coral structure where the water flows freely. Once they have secured a grip upon the coral, they unfold their feathery arms like painted fans and begin feeding. These creatures are particularly sensitive to light, for when an under-water torch is beamed at them they quickly curl their arms. If the light remains the animal will climb down from the coral and return to its hiding place. However, if the flashlight is turned off the crinoid slowly spreads its arms into an intricate, fragile work of art.

48. Grape Algae *Caulerpa racemosa* (Forskål) • Orange Lace Ascidians *Didemnum candidum* Savigny • Crustose Coralline Algae and Sponges • Life size • Ulach pass, Ngcheangel islands • 80 feet • 2 August 1971

This cluster of grape algae is growing under a ledge. Algae are abundant in tropical seas, but on coral reefs they are usually less conspicuous than many of the animals. Species of algae exist as phytoplankton suspended in the water, as symbionts with corals, ascidians, and clams, or as encrusting layers over dead coral rubble. To the human observer, algae are most conspicuous in the ledge environments where species are more likely to resemble singular entities. They look like clusters of grapes or little leaves and are usually the color of something that contains chlorophyll. In other areas, clumps of algae grow around the base of corals, particularly the staghorn varieties, where they are probably better able to withstand wave action or at least use the base of the corals for support.

49. Fern Hydroid *Macrorhynchia* sp. • Staghorn Coral *Acropora* sp. • Algae • 1-1/4 times life size • Pass reef, Ngeruangel reef • 35 feet • 31 July 1971

Occasionally, fern hydroids are found in lagoon environments. Most often, however, they live where the water contains less sediment. At the same time, they do not inhabit areas that sustain strong currents or wave action. The combination of these two factors somewhat limits the distribution of this particular animal. The wide pass at Ngeruangel reef is subjected to a gentle current of clean ocean waters. Consequently, more fern hydroids are living at Ngeruangel within the inner pass than at any other area in Belau which I explored. As seen in this photograph, fern hydroids most often grow attached to dead coral skeletons or old coral rocks overgrown with a layer of reddish brown algae.

50. Like the passes at the atolls and barrier reefs, channels also cut through many of the fringing reefs adjacent to the main islands. I think of these channels as inner passes. Along the eastern edge of Belau there are large gaps in the outer barrier reef where the open ocean comes closest to the land. As the fringing reefs of the land continued growing over thousands of years, they formed a barrier separating the ocean from the lagoon. Simultaneously, the ebb and flow of water across the reef found natural paths that evolved to their present form. As this aerial view from 500 feet shows, Ngel pass is a distinct channel through the fringing reef even though the reef is essentially adjacent to the land. This pass is one of two eastern entrances to Ngederrak lagoon, the open body of water at the top center of the photograph. The area in the foreground to the left of Ngel pass is Ngederrak reef. In the distance behind Ngederrak reef is the northeastern end of Ngeruktabel island. On the right of Ngel pass, adjacent to Ngeruptachel island, is a continuation of the fringing reef. It is easy to see how the reef is really a part of Ngeruptachel island which, in a past age, was itself a reef of living corals. In the center of Ngeruptachel island is Risong cove. The smaller Jellyfish Coves (not seen in this photograph) are inner extensions of Risong cove. In the distance on the right of Ngederrak lagoon is Ngemelachel island with the white buildings of the wharf area clearly visible. The gap at the far end of Ngederrak lagoon is Teongel pass, the western entrance to the lagoon area. Teongel pass separates Kuabsngas point of Ngeruktabel island on the left from Bedulyaus point of Ngerchol island on the right. The distance between the fringing reef in the foreground and Teongel pass in the distance is about four and one-half nautical miles

as a tropic bird flies…assuming it flies as straight as a crow. (15 October 1971)

51. Silver Crinoid *Cenometra bella* Hartlaub • Cotton Candy Coral *Siphonogorgia godeffroyi* Kölliker • Life size • Kesebekuu pass reef, Kesebekuu pass • 30 feet • 6 November 1967

Like Ngel pass, Kesebekuu pass also facilitates the tidal flow into Ngederrak lagoon from the east. On the north it is bounded by Ngederrak reef and on the south by Kesebekuu pass reef. Kesebekuu pass is a well-defined channel through the reef from the open ocean and is therefore the main entry into Ngederrak lagoon for large ships. Even though most of the ships use it, the traffic as of 1973 is not heavy enough to destroy the marine life. Lovely alcyonarians and crinoids, along with other creatures, still inhabit the coral walls of the pass. These animals trap the plankton of an incoming tide in the same way as their relatives do in areas less frequented by man and his machines. However, the marine life closer to the wharf has not fared as well. If "civilization" makes greater demands on the lagoon, the marine life will be supplanted increasingly by beer cans and rubber tires.

Occasionally I encounter people who confuse the beauty of the subject matter with photographic quality. Invariably, they like my underwater photographs best because they are of strangely beautiful, unfamiliar subjects. They seem less enthusiastic about a photograph of some more familiar subject such as a bird in flight or a human face. Somehow they value the familiar less. I always explain to them that for me all life is miraculous and that each species is a wondrous creation. If only the unfamiliar excites them, it will be just a matter of time before they lose interest in sea creatures and, in so doing, lose more of the meaning of life.

52. Like the passes, the lagoons do not have distinct boundaries. In certain areas the lagoon is only slightly separated from the open ocean and therefore many marine organisms found on the outer reefs also exist in areas usually thought of as the lagoon environment. This is true because similar physical conditions occur in both environments in some areas and, of course, even the extremes of the various environments do not differ enough to prevent a partial invasion by species from other zones. Salt water crocodiles, for instance, primarily frequent the mangrove areas, but are also found in the open ocean and even in the marine lakes.

Nevertheless, the lagoons do have certain characteristics which distinguish them from the passes and outer reefs. It is safest, though, to think of areas plurally, and in that way the lagoons can be further subdivided into those areas closer to the open ocean and into other areas less exposed to the effects of cleaner water and stronger wave action. If an obvious characterisitic is needed to distinguish the lagoons from the outer reefs, it would probably be the abundance of shallow-water corals growing just beneath the surface of the water. Due to their locations, the lagoons are somewhat protected environments and consequently the corals there are more delicately sculptured. In fact, the nature of the coral structures can be used to determine the degree to which a particular environment is sheltered from violent ocean storms.

This photograph affords a view of the fringing reef on the more sheltered west side of Moir islands. Here the coral is much more protected from the open ocean. The tiny mushroom-shaped rock island on the left and the larger more distant rock island are both of limestone origin. In some ancient age, the limestone was clothed in the delicate hues of living corals; now it is arrayed in the lush deep green of terrestrial vegetation. (26 May 1971)

53. Fluted Giant Clam *Tridacna squamosa* Lamarck • Algae *Codium* sp. • Life size • Ngeremdiu reef, White Cliff, Ngeruktabel island • 35 feet • 6 October 1970

While thorny oysters live primarily on the outer reefs, the fluted giant clams are most abundant in the lagoons. Like most sedentary animals, these clams filter plankton and organic debris from water they pump through their bodies.

When we realize that plankton are the children of many of the sea's creatures including the giant clam, we may wonder how species survive. It is known that some animals do feed on their own offspring under varying circumstances. However, it seems to me that a fascinating study could be made to see if plankton feeders such as clams are selective in what they capture and eat. For instance, it is possible that giant clams or corals feed on larval forms *other* than their own species.

Nevertheless, it is not difficult to understand how animals can collectively feed on their own larvae and still survive as a species. The sea's children, the plankton, are generally far more numerous than their parents, thus creating an overall balance. It is impossible to have more plankton feeders than plankton since, by their very feeding habits, the adults limit their numbers. When an adult clam dies or is eaten, there is a momentarily unoccupied space. If the new arrival is not a tiny clam, it will be a coral, an ascidian, or some other reef creature—which is why the face of the reef is constantly changing.

54. Golden-crested Damselfish *Abudefduf xanthonotus* (Bleeker) • Staghorn Coral *Acropora formosa* (Dana) • Life size • East reef, Macharchar islands • 10 feet • 7 September 1969

Every time one creature eats, another dies. Still, an overall balance exists wherein each species maintains a certain stability. This charming little damselfish lives among the spires of the staghorn coral and, watching for larger predators, utilizes the network of coral for its own protection by darting among the branches when danger threatens.

The east reef of Macharchar islands is protected by a barrier reef farther off shore, but Macharchar's fringing reef is still fairly open to strong wave action. Consequently, even though the staghorn coral atop the reef is quite graceful in structure, its architecture is more spartan than baroque.

55. Periodically during the course of each year, the tops of the reefs are exposed to the air. Every day in Belau there are normally two high tides and two low tides, alternating high and low, approximately every six hours. Depending upon the position of the sun and moon in relation to the earth, there are two neap tides and two spring tides each month. The ideal neap tide occurs when the sun and moon are at right angles to each other in the sky. This conjunction tends to minimize the rise and fall of the tide so that the low tide is not very low and the neap high tide is accordingly not very high. On the other hand, spring tides occur when the sun and moon are lined up and therefore exerting a pull on the earth in the same direction. The sun and moon can be on opposite sides of the earth at full moon, or they can be lined up on the same side at new moon when the sun's brightness outshines the moon which is rendered too pale to be seen at midday. At such times the combined gravity of the moon and sun exert their greatest pull on the ocean waters because each is more nearly complementing the gravitational pull of the other. Thus, the oscillation of the ocean water is intensified, causing lower low tides and higher high tides. The peaks of the tidal changes come later each day because the tides are really lunar-dominated. The moon does not keep pace with the daily revolution of the earth and consequently causes a tidal delay of fifty minutes each and every day. The sun further alters the tides by minimizing the highs and lows as in neap tides, or maximizing them as in spring tides. Since the earth also turns on its axis as it revolves around the sun during the course of a year, the sun is in a different position in relationship to the equator each day. Consequently, when the sun is highest overhead at any one place on the earth, it is exerting its greatest gravitational pull on that place. During spring and early summer in Belau, which is slightly north of the equator, the new moon and the sun exert the greatest combined gravitational pull on the water. If, in Belau, there is an average or mean low tide, then at those times of the year during the greatest extremes of tide the ocean level will periodically drop considerably below this mean. It is at these times

that minus tides occur. Just as with the average tides, there is a constant variation that holds true for the extra-low tides. The combined forces of the sun and moon increase day by day until they reach a peak that causes the most extreme minus tide and then as the moon alters its position the minus tide lessens with each succeeding day.

Corals cannot live out of water very long. However, for most of the year, not only in Belau but in other areas of the tropics, a minus tide is not a daily occurrence. Therefore, corals can and do grow near the surface of the mean low water mark and remain submerged. Only on those days of minus tides are the delicate corals of the reef tops exposed to the air. This photograph of a fringing reef in Macharchar lagoon, at the north end of Macharchar islands, was taken two days after the new moon. For two days prior to this, the low tide was even lower and the corals were more exposed for a greater length of time. As is readily seen in this photograph, some of the coral polyps have either partially or totally disintegrated and the white skeletal branches are exposed. The coral's exposure to the air may only last for an hour to ninety minutes, but since the extra-low tide occurs during the day, the sun may be shining or it may be raining. If the sun were shining as was the situation when this photograph was made, then the corals would suffer from desiccation. If, on the other hand, it were a rainy day, the corals would suffer from the physical force of the falling raindrops and the lack of salt content. The fresh rainwater kills the thin layer of living flesh. Although considerable natural violence occurs on this planet, the ocean is still a relatively gentle world and those creatures that live in it have adapted to its ways. Corals have not adapted to living above water constantly, but some of them are still capable of living just below its surface with the hazards such living entails. From my own observations, the exposed areas of the coral skeleton where the polyps were at least partly or totally destroyed are soon overgrown with new polyps reproduced from the colony. From the photograph it is easy to see that not all the coral branches are white ...much of the colony is still a healthy brownish color. Four months after this photograph was made, the white areas of the staghorn coral branches were newly covered with living polyps. I let my boat drift over the submerged reef top and I saw no sign of white or dead algae-covered skeletons.

From this photograph, taken about mid-afternoon at low tide, it is possible to sense the great abundance of life in all its vitality. One can almost feel the emergence of the land from the sea. Ngeremeaus island with its white sand beach is of biological origin. To its left with another sand beach is Ngeanges island and on the distant right are the Beab islands. Rising above them in the far distance is the southeastern ridge of Ngeruktabel island. All these limestone islands were once living reefs and in another way are living still. (26 May 1971)

56. Black Coral *Antipathes bifaria* Brook • Tropic Sky Ascidians *Clavelina* sp. • 1-3/4 times life size • Beab pass reef, Beab island • 90 feet • 28 October 1967

While some corals grow slightly below the surface of the water, others live far down the sides of the reefs. This black coral is growing on the bottom of the pass on the north side of Beab island. A luminous cluster of tiny blue ascidians lives on the black coral. Each ascidian has two openings which serve as the ends of a siphon. The animal beats hair-like cilia within the gill basket in its body, creating a current of water that enters the mouth opening, passes through the slits of the gill basket, and exits at the second opening, the atrium. The plankton in the water is trapped as it passes through the gill basket and then is digested in the ascidian's intestine. As the name implies, the gill basket also serves the animal as a respiratory organ. Ascidians can multiply by division and by sexual reproduction. This little cluster probably began as one individual and slowly multiplied. Years later I tried to revisit it to see the results of its continued growth but, unfortunately, I couldn't find the black coral tree again.

57. Looking south into Macharchar lagoon with the fringing reef of Ngchelobel island in the foreground, this photograph shows the diminishing minus effect of the tides. The picture was made the day after a prior photograph (plate 55) and the corals are not uncovered as completely as on the previous day. However, it has been raining and those few coral spires that show above the surface are denuded. It is interesting to note that this large coral formation is richly covered with various species of stony corals. If compared with the similarly situated coral head seen atop the outer barrier that borders Ngerumekaol pass in front of Ulong island, it becomes apparent that the more protected corals of the fringing reef of Macharchar lagoon can indeed grow closer to the surface than those on the outer barrier reef where the more violent wave action greatly restricts the growth. (27 May 1971)

58. Red Encrusting Sponge *Microciona eurypa* (de Laubenfels)? • Christmas Tree Hydroids • 1-3/4 times life size • Fringing reef, Macharchar lagoon, Ngchelobel island • 40 feet • 12 September 1969

This red sponge and the white hydroids have overgrown a section of wire coral. The coral's enduring skeleton is capable of supporting the tenants and on each side of them (not seen in this photograph), the wire coral is alive. In the sea there always seems to be this interrelationship of life forms. One form dies a little and another is born, like changing expressions on a human face.

When photographing this intricate community of red and white, I only made two exposures. Upon returning home and viewing the developed film, it was like a childhood memory of Christmas. I felt the need to reinforce the experience and when I returned to Belau nine months later, I visited the reef again. Seeing the wire coral, I was shocked. The coral was still living but the crimson sponge had died and almost all the winter-white hydroid Christmas trees were gone.

59. Peacock Lionfish *Pterois volitans* (Linnaeus) • Giant Finger Sponge *Raphidophlus cervicornis* Thiele • Life size • Mutremdiu point lagoon, Uchelbeluu reef • 60 feet • 11 August 1971

Although lionfishes do live in the passes and on the outer reef fronts, they seem to be more common within the lagoon areas. With their array of delicate fins, they usually live in the deeper waters where surface waves and surge are minimal. During the day, a lionfish usually hides under a coral head. On cloudy days or at dusk, it emerges and glides slowly among the coral branches, then stops and waits with head slightly downward. Nearby a group of cardinalfish congregates around an adjacent coral head. As the evening progresses, the cardinalfish increasingly ignore the predator. The lionfish inches forward. The cardinalfish relax and become a little more preoccupied while feeding on passing plankton. In the oncoming darkness, a single cardinalfish drifts a little away from the crowd and, as day becomes night, one fish becomes part of another.

60. Fluted Giant Clam *Tridacna squamosa* Lamarck • Cardinalfish *Archamia fucata* (Cantor) • Red Encrusting Sponge • 3/4 life size • Patch reef, Ngederrak lagoon, Ngeruktabel island • 15 feet • 23 September 1969

This fluted giant clam's psychedelic mantle is differently patterned from its predecessor's. It is easy to see the contrast of pattern despite the fact that the basic colors of the mantles are similar. However, there are other fluted clams that are green, electric blue, brown, rust, navy blue, pink, and gold through all varying combinations and patterns that would put the human fingerprint to shame. Of course, the truth of the matter is that each and every manifestation of life is wonderfully unique, however rigid the guidelines for existence.

61. Cobalt Sea Star *Linckia laevigata* (Linnaeus) • Ruffled Algae *Padina japonica* Yamada • Staghorn Coral Skeletons *Acropora* sp. • Encrusting Algae • Life size •
Kesebekuu pass reef, Mekeald lagoon, Ngeruktabel island • 40 feet • 27 August 1969

Many sea stars only emerge at night to feed. Others, such as this cobalt sea star, range over the reef during the day. It is thought that its blue color protects it from the rays of the sunlight. Although this sea star was photographed in forty feet of water, the species is more commonly found on the reef tops in very shallow water among the corals and on the grass flats where the sunlight is even brighter. It moves very slowly and evidently feeds on organic matter, including sponges that encrust dead corals. The reef, of course, is not a solid mass of living corals. There are areas of rich coral growth interspersed with areas of dead coral and sand bottom. The cobalt sea star is most commonly found in these bottom areas rich in microscopic life.

62. Salt and Pepper Sea Urchin *Echinothrix calamaris* (Pallas) • Turtle Grass *Enhalus acoroides* (L.f) Steud • 1-3/4 times life size • Ngederrak reef, Ngederrak lagoon • 4 feet • 11 October 1967

During the day this sea urchin hides on the underside of dead coral heads that litter the shallow waters of the reef top. Here it keeps company with cone shells, cowries, brittle stars, and other nocturnal creatures that wait until dark to emerge. Then they come out upon the reef top and forage for organic matter in the sand among the turtle grass. Other sea urchins are active during the daytime but even these species partially re-create the cover of night. They pick up bits of debris such as pebbles and turtle grass and hold them on the top of their spines with their tube feet. This strange garb probably helps to shade them from the sun's rays as well as to camouflage them from would-be predators.

63. String Sponge *Xestospongia exiqua* (Kirkpatrick) • Ruffled Algae *Padina japonica* Yamada • Green Algae *Dictyota patens* J. Agardh • Staghorn Coral Skeletons *Acropora* sp. • 1-3/4 times life size • Kesebekuu pass reef, Mekeald lagoon, Ngeruktabel island • 30 feet • 21 June 1970

The sea has its graveyards, but they are living graveyards and therefore not really cemeteries at all. Only man seems to have a misguided reverence for the dead to the extent that he feels the need to try to preserve forever that which ultimately can never be preserved. If the seeming finality of death is somehow held off by preservatives and air-tight concrete-enclosed metal containers, in another way this kind of preservation is more deathly than any natural form of dying. In the sea, as in the rest of nature, life passes to life with death being nothing more than another moment in a state of perpetual transition. In the truest sense, there is no such thing as death. As e. e. cummings wrote:

when (instead of stopping to think) you

begin to feel of it, dying
's miraculous
why?   be

cause dying is
perfectly natural; perfectly
putting
it mildly lively...

In the sea, if the skeletons of corals remain, they are soon clothed in the greens and browns of algae and again transformed "into something rich and strange." A creature rarely dies of old age in the sea. Those that are weak, sick, or disabled are more subject to predators. But whatever the form of transition, nothing remains unchanged. As soon as a plant or animal is no longer a living entity, the countless bacteria of the sea begin to feed on it and break down the cells into their basic components. The tissues become nitrates, carbon dioxide, and phosphates again. The substrate of the reef is rich in bacteria that thrive on the constant rain of dead and dying organisms. Here the basic elements of life are released from their temporary housings and returned to the sea where they can be used by the phyto-plankton to become the living...again.

This photograph shows how living things build on the old skeletons of corals and how sediment fills in the open spaces, consolidating the substrate of the reef. Over centuries and centuries, the reef grows layer by layer, a superorganism that is, more truly than any melodist of a Grecian Urn, "piping songs forever new...forever young...."

64. Pincushion Sea Star *Culcita novaeguineae* Müller & Troschel • Algae-encrusted Staghorn Coral Skeletons *Acropora* sp. • 3/4 life size • Patch reef, Mekeald lagoon, Ngeruktabel island • 40 feet • 21 May 1970

Here is another echinoderm that is sometimes active during the daylight hours. It looks more like a pincushion than a sea star because as an adult it lacks distinct arms. However, its complex anatomical organization is readily apparent when one views the animal's underside. The five radiating rows of its tube feet reveal its five pointed radial symmetry. With a little practice one can see that the tips of the "arms" are pointed at approximately one, three, five, eight, and eleven o'clock. The pincushion sea stars are another species that never "dresses" quite the same twice. Like the fluted giant clams, each sea star has its own combination of colors and I am always amazed by the artistry with which the colors are selected.

This sea star has a tough outer covering that probably protects it from predators (not to mention the fact that it would be a big mouthful for most of the reef's inhabitants). As an adult it may very well have natural enemies but I wouldn't know what they are. Nevertheless, during the day I have often seen them wedged partly under a coral head or between coral rocks which would indicate that these creatures do concern themselves with self-defense. The pincushion sea star, like the crown-of-thorns, feeds extensively on corals, particularly those colonies with smooth surfaces.

65. Lizardfish *Synodus variegatus* (Lacépède) • Ruffled Algae *Padina japonica* Yamada • Algae-encrusted Staghorn Coral Skeletons • 1-1/2 times life size • Kesebekuu pass reef, Mekeald lagoon, Ngeruktabel island • 35 feet • 18 October 1967

Many times I have seen lizardfish, in twos and threes, perched on a coral projection waiting for the right moment to attack an unsuspecting fish. However, in this instance, these lizardfish are probably a pair that may be involved in some stage of the reproductive act. When I photographed them, their colors seemed the same to me. At a glance, they both seemed to be a mottled brown color like the fish in the foreground. When viewing the photograph later, I was amazed to discover that both fish were not the same color. The water filters out the red rays of the sun, and at forty feet reds do look brown. Even so, I have photographed numerous lizardfish in many surroundings. Always, if there were more than one, their colors would be very similar to their background and to each other like the two on the outer reef (Plate 29). Consequently, it is possible that the red color of the one lizardfish may be distinguishable enough to its companion. If indeed they are a pair, this subtle color difference could serve as a pairing or sexual signal, while to a passing fish or predator the pair still blends unobtrusively with their algae-encrusted coral environment.

66. Remora *Echeneis naucrates* Linnaeus • 1/2 life size • Kesebekuu pass reef, Mekeald lagoon, Ngeruktabel island • 40 feet • 6 September 1969

Remoras are known for their symbiotic relationships with sharks, rays, turtles, and other large marine animals. The remora's body is beautifully adapted to co-exist with these larger ocean creatures. The remora's head and suction disk are dramatic examples of the workings of evolution. The structure of the disk demonstrates how one appendage, the dorsal fin, was phylogenetically molded into another for the better survival of this animal. Unlike most midwater fishes, the remora's dorsal surface, including the disk, is flattened. This shape enables the remora to attach easily to the host, becoming almost a part of its body. If the reader looks at the photograph of the remora attached to the black-tip shark, it becomes apparent that the hitchhiker, is not much of a burden. The remora swims right along with the shark, conforming to its undulating movements. Like its host, it is dynamically designed to offer the least resistance to the water. The remora also seems to keep the shark relatively free of external parasites even though its normal diet probably consists of bits of flesh that the shark leaves behind in its violent feeding activities.

Occasionally, while swimming in the lagoons, I have looked up to discover a large remora circling me. No doubt it is looking for a host. Since remoras have adapted to living with much larger animals, they seem to be more curious than fearful. If I remain still, the remora circles me. If I try to swim away from it, the animal follows me. If I advance, it retreats. Sometimes there are two together, one swimming beneath the other in true remora fashion. Quite often the remoras living within the lagoons have damaged tail fins and appear sickly. It seems to me that perhaps they have become old and have not been able to keep up with their sharks and therefore have entered the lagoons where they live until they are eaten or eventually die.

Once, at Ulach pass, I photographed a leopard shark that was accompanied by a small twelve inch-long remora. The shark was resting on the sand and the remora was attached upsidedown to the top of the shark's head. When I approached, the remora swam away from the shark and circled around me. After a minute, the little fish swam back to the shark, but instead of re-attaching itself it settled to the bottom near the shark's head. As they lay there side by side, I couldn't help but feel that their relationship was more than mere necessity...unless companionship is as necessary as sunlight and food.

67. Skunk Clownfish *Amphiprion perideraion* Bleeker • Sea Anemone *Radianthus ritteri* (Kwietniewski) • 1-1/4 times life size • Kesebekuu pass reef, Mekeald lagoon, Ngeruktabel island • 25 feet • 16 September 1969

Skunk clownfishes and their anemones are most common on the outer reef fronts in water forty to fifty feet deep and also within the lagoon areas where there is a moderately strong current. The currents in the passes are, in most instances, too strong for the anemones and these animals rarely live there. Nevertheless, everything is a matter of degree. Occasionally, the overall environment is less of a determining factor than are the particular circumstances of a certain habitat. Therefore, quite often there are exceptions to the rule.

This anemone traps plankton with its expanded tentacles and later transfers the food to its mouth. The skunk clowns live with the anemone and have acquired immunity from the stinging cells of their host's tentacles. Consequently, the comical little fish can swim vigorously among the tentacles without triggering the stinging nematocysts that would kill other fishes their size. The clowns can even "mouth" the tentacles and often do so in their feeding activities. The clowns regularly swim above the anemone where they catch the passing plankton, but they also feed off the tentacles and particularly at the anemone's mouth where wastes are discarded. In this way, the clowns help rid the anemone of its waste products. Of course, for the clowns, the waste is food and the adults carefully guard the supply. There is actually a ranking order. When the adults are otherwise occupied, the juveniles steal to the mouth of the anemone and snatch a bit of food. If discovered, they are chased away. Each clownfish in turn chases a smaller fish. In this way, the food supply is not totally depleted and the anemone is able to support the family of skunk clowns.

One scientist recently discovered that the skunk clownfish juveniles are really not as young as one would think from looking at them. The scientist studied a family of skunk clowns for about six months and then removed the adults from the anemone. Within a short period of two months, the growth rate of the remaining juveniles accelerated tremendously. Evidently the ranking system prevents the smaller clowns from eating enough to grow to maturity until there is a vacancy in the upper ranks. In this way, the anemone is able to sustain a larger number of fish which in turn are ready and able to replace adults that die. This system helps to perpetuate the species within the framework of its symbiotic relationship.

68. Leather Coral *Lobophytum pauciflorum* (Ehrenberg) • Life size • Kesebekuu pass reef, Mekeald lagoon, Ngeruktabel island • 30 feet • 17 May 1970

The spires of this soft-bodied coral rise from their common base like New York City's skyscrapers seen from the air. In many ways a coral reef and individual corals are like skyscrapers. The space on a reef, like Manhattan Island, is limited and of necessity the corals build upward to take advantage of the area above them. The size, shape, and spacing of the coral spires in relation to one another allow for a maximum of body surface-to-water contact with the result that each polyp is able to breathe and feed. In this photograph, all the tiny white polyps of the leather coral are feeding while the tide flows. When the current ceases, the polyps will disappear within the golden brown flesh and the whole colony will partially contract until it is time to feed again. Leather corals are paricularly abundant in areas where the currents are quite strong. These animals are very resilient and can withstand surges and wave action. Consequently they are very common in the passes.

69. Ragged Chalice Coral *Oxypora lacera* Verrill • 1/3 life size • East Cove reef, Mekeald lagoon, Ngeruktabel island • 30 feet • 6 November 1970

Deeper within the lagoon the current diminishes to a gentle flow. In Mekeald lagoon the reef is much more protected by the high ridges of Ngeruktabel island and the nearby shallow reefs that break the open ocean swells. Here the stony corals begin to attain an elaborateness of form not found in species that live on the outer reef tops or in areas of greater water turbulence. This young coral colony grows upward from a very small base in comparison with the colony's overall structure. In the calm, slowly moving waters of this particular reef, its chalice-like structure enables it to take maximum advantage of the conditions of its habitat. The shape of the colony is also an adaptation to the current and the sun. The symbiotic algae within its tissues use the energy from the sunlight to change the wastes from each polyp into carbohydrates, proteins, fats, and oxygen. This process of photosynthesis, with its rapid exchange of gases and carbohydrates, allows the polyps to live very close to one another. In contrast, the corals that live in very deep water or under ledges do not contain algae in their body tissues. Like the tube corals of The Great Reef, they are only able to form small aggregates of polyps. Consequently it is the algae-storing corals, such as this ragged chalice coral, and calcareous algae that are the major reef builders.

70. Vivaldi Staghorn Coral *Acropora polymorpha* Brook • 1/2 life size • Patch reef, Mekeald lagoon, Ngeruktabel island • 35 feet • 21 May 1970

Compared with some other staghorn corals, this species is considerably more elaborate. The close proximity of its many branches would make it a sail in the wind were it not for the gentle environment in which it lives. Like a sea fan, this coral is growing vertically against the horizontal direction of the current, exposing the greatest possible surface to the passing water which provides the colony with food, oxygen, and minerals. This staghorn coral also lives on the east reef of Macharchar islands not far from its spartanly structured relative. However, the shallow reef top at Macharchar is much less protected. On days when the wind is blowing from the northeast, the waves surge

over the reef and the corals are subjected to physical forces to which they must conform—or perish. Here, the Vivaldi staghorn coral grows upward only a little before curving horizontally…a gesture of humility to the forces that shape all living things, including man.

71. Candy Cane Sea Star *Nardoa novaecaledoniae* (Perrier) • Christmas Tree Coral *Acropora procumbens* (Brook)? • Pink Encrusting Sponge • 4/5 life size • Patch reef, Ngel pass, Ngederrak lagoon • 20 feet • 22 August 1971

Late one afternoon, just before sunset, I was photographing a Moorish Idol as it flitted among the branches of a coral. During one free moment, I turned around and encountered this jewel-like candy cane sea star. It had been hiding all day in the intertwined network of dead coral branches below and was now emerging to feed. Unfortunately, I was busy photographing the fish and only stopped long enough to make two photographs of the sea star. I was too preoccupied to watch its feeding activities, so I've no idea if it feeds on coral. The christmas tree coral in the foreground has been partly eaten and its branches on the right are completely denuded. Predation from sea stars is one way corals are killed, their skeletons becoming part of the substrate. Occasionally I have seen a small isolated coral stripped completely of flesh. The crown-of-thorns definitely preys upon corals. Most of the time, a totally-stripped coral is the work of this animal since, as a large sea star, it has the capability. However, just as often I have come upon formations of large staghorn corals that have been what I would call "grazed." The upper surface of quite a number of the branches have had the flesh eaten from the skeleton but the remaining coral polyps on the sides and undersurface are in good condition. On close examination, one can see how the uneaten part of the colony is growing back over the grazed area. If the crown-of-thorns strips a coral colony bare as a matter of course during population explosions, it is just as likely that this sea star normally grazes randomly and only occasionally strips a few branches or a small coral completely bare. It seems reasonable that the slow-growing corals could not survive the feeding activities of the crown-of-thorns if the sea star always stripped every colony bare or if the still-living part of the colony was never able to repair the damage it sustained.

In another area of the world I have observed and photographed a species of coral in various stages of repair after different colonies have been grazed by parrotfish. On one newly grazed colony, the teeth of the parrotfish had left rows and patches of white coral skeleton amid the still-living polyps. On other nearby colonies of the same species (ones not so recently grazed) regeneration was in full progress. A slight coloring over the teeth-marked areas was evidence that repair of lost tissue was taking place and on closer inspection I could see that the partly destroyed calices were being reconstructed. As the new layer of flesh acquired a greater concentration of symbiotic algae within its tissues, its light color would eventually darken to that of the surrounding polyps which had escaped the feeding activities of the parrotfishes.

On another colony that had sustained heavy damage, a thin layer of algae had overgrown some of the bare patches. When I encounter a sponge or ascidian growing in the center of a coral colony, I know that at some time in the colony's past something disrupted its uniform growth. When a parrotfish grazes a coral there is the possibility that the larva of a sponge will settle there and begin its sessile life. What occurs is a matter of chance, dependent upon the degree of destruction of the coral colony, the timing of the new arrival, and its ability to withstand the reconstruction of the coral polyps. Even though a thin layer of algae may rapidly cover a bare patch of coral skeleton, it can be supplanted later by the closing ring of coral polyps that are new additions to the old colony. Or a new arrival such as a sponge may hold its own and even eliminate more coral polyps around it as it grows.

72. I had never seen the "Land of the Fairies" until I saw the Ngerukuid islands from the air. Translated, Ngerukuid means seventy and these seventy islands are a nature preserve not always respected by every Belauan. In the near distance, atop the western barrier reef, are the Kmekumer islands. This total island complex, seen from an altitude of 700 feet, is just inside the barrier reef. The nearest passes are northward near Ulong and southward at Ngemelis. Consequently, the coral growth around these limestone islands is relatively sparse because of a lack of clean sea water in the vicinity. For all their beauty, the seventy islands are off the mainstream of ocean life. Here we see the beginning hints of secluded coves where life seems to move at a slower pace. Viewing these lovely islands, which are really parts of a single structure, one somehow senses the unhurried rise and fall of centuries. (15 October 1971)

73. Some things are the work of centuries, others are a day's work. At Ngcheangel atoll, the western shores of all four low lying islands border the shallow lagoon. To the north, the long white beach of Ngcheangel island stretches in the distance. The sandbar in the foreground is part of the northern end of Ngerebelas island. At low tide the ridges of the sandbar, separate at the surface, are still connected underwater. Many islands in the lagoon mirror these protruding ridges even though the lagoon bottom may be 110 feet beneath the surface and their present form evolved over centuries instead of hours. Here, on a sunny blue-sky day, the wind and gentle waves have sculptured the sand into graceful ridges that have all the beauty of the most exquisite work of art but, like a child's sand castle, will disappear with the incoming tide. (1 August 1971)

74. One of the largest rock island complexes is situated on the western side of Ngeruktabel island, seen from an altitude of 800 feet. To the right in the near distance is Kekereltoi (Little Pass) seen as a small gap in the ridge of Ngeruktabel island, which continues to the left across the entire photograph. In the far distant center are the Ngerukuid islands. To the left, beyond the ridge of Ngeruktabel, is the Macharchar islands complex. In contrast to the aerial view of Ngerukuid islands (Plate 72), where the surrounding water is shallow, the water seen here is 110 feet deep and the islands are larger, higher, and more greatly separated by water. Belau's tuna fishing fleet uses this area to catch and store live sardines, the tiny silver fish used as bait. The waters of the baitgrounds are completely surrounded on all sides by these islands which shelter the floating bait wells from storms. During the Japanese occupation of Belau, ships were anchored in the deeper waters of the lagoon. Many of these Japanese ships are now on the bottom as a result of the 1941-45 war. At the entrance to the bait grounds area, one such wreck is sitting upright in 110 feet of water. The bow is blown out and the deck that once supported human feet is now covered with a layer of fine white sediment. The rails and the sides are adorned with delicate corals and the rich silent colors of encrusting sponges. The yawning deck "holds" and narrow doorways now lead only to darkness. The wreck has become part of the reef and is covered with a thin layer of life. This life sustains smaller fishes which in turn sustain schools of larger fishes that seem eager to receive visitors from above. The wreck is isolated and those fishes that inhabit it seem destined never to leave. In a sense this ship, like the blue Earth spinning in the darkness of space, is a living prison. Perhaps its inhabitants feel no need to escape but their children are still entrusted to the pull of the tides like an eternal hope born of necessity. If "hope" has too anthropomorphic a meaning, still all of life on sunken ships and planets alike arrived from somewhere to live and leave again. If, as we define it, a fish is not capable of hope, somewhere in its genes is contained that necessary expression of its existence. To deny it would be to deny it in ourselves. (15 October 1971)

75. Golden Jacks *Caranx speciosus* (Forskål) • 1/2 life size • The Wreck, Bait Grounds Entrance, Ngeruktabel island • 75 feet • 16 May 1971

These four golden jacks are members of a larger school numbering about thirty. They have lived on the wreck for years and primarily feed on the debris, algae, and small organisms that grow on its superstructure. They are very busy feeders, and as a group remain in one spot for little more than fifteen or twenty seconds before hurrying on to the next location. Watching them, I get the impression that there are not enough hours in the day for them to feed. I sense that frantic atmosphere associated with crowded city dwellers who rely on too many artificial arrangements to survive.

76. Fluted Oysters *Pycnodonta hyotis* (Linnaeus) • Opal Bubble Coral *Plerogyra sinuosa* (Dana) • Mangrove Mussels *Septifer bilocularis* (Linnaeus) • 4/5 life size • The Wreck, Bait Grounds Entrance, Ngeruktabel island • 75 feet • 1 June 1971

On this 400-foot-long wreck, marine life flourishes on the surface area of the hull, particularly the starboard side between a depth of seventy and ninety feet. The railing of the ship, about seventy feet below the surface, is also heavily encrusted with organisms that continue to grow down the sides of the hull. At a depth of 100 feet, a great concentration of sediment is suspended in the water like a thick fog bank resting on the floor of the lagoon. Evidently the ship acts as a barrier to the flow of the current, causing a somewhat stagnant condition and a marked decrease in the encrusting life from this level to the bottom, where the side of the ship disappears into the soft ooze.

Seventy-five feet below the surface, these fluted oysters live in the area richest in encrusting life. Here the metal surface of the hull is completely covered with algae and other marine animals such as the smaller mussels and bubble coral. Even the fluted oyster's shell is home for a tiny fish and many transparent anemones.

77. Batfish *Platax teira* (Forskål) • 1/4 life size • The Wreck, Bait Grounds Entrance, Ngeruktabel island • 15 feet • 22 June 1970

Along with the golden jacks, the wreck supports a school of barracudas and another larger school of jacks. There is also a small community of batfish that inhabit it. Up until the summer of 1971, these batfish congregated around the top of the forward mast which came to within five feet of the surface at low tide. Here the batfish would swim near the surface and feed on the larger conglomerates of organic matter, plankton, and also the invertebrate life encrusting the mast. In fact, the mast was a focal point for their activities until the tuna fishermen took notice of it, decided it was a hazard to navigation, and had the top thirty feet blown off. Now the batfish "space station" is gone and when I encounter these fish elsewhere around the wreck, they are no longer as trusting. Consequently, the memory of my first encounter with them is the one I prefer to keep. The batfish circled around me with obvious curiosity as I hovered in the water fifteen feet below the surface. My interest in them was photographic while their interest in me was apparently gastronomical. As I moved about in the water, my hair swayed like algae in a surge of current. It wasn't long before my photographic activities were interrupted by one hungry batfish tugging on my hair.

78. Fluorescent Daisy Coral *Alveopora allingi* Hoffmeister • Black Coral *Antipathes arborea* Dana • Crustose Coralline Algae • 1-3/4 times life size • The Wreck, Bait Grounds Entrance, Ngeruktabel island • 80 feet • 10 October 1970

Like a small bouquet of flowers, this daisy coral grows on the wreck in the most heavily encrusted zone of life. This particular coral's polyps are much larger than the white skeleton to which they are attached. These large-polyped colonies only exist in the calm depths where the current moves slowly. The slightest displacement of water greatly disturbs their delicate arrangement.

Some daisy corals, as well as other basically solitary deep water species, often glow with pale fluorescent colors. The sunlight contains ultraviolet radiation and these rays excite chemical substances within the coral polyps, causing them to fluoresce in varying hues. Any one color is determined by chemical groups known as flavines, pterines, or urobilines in the form of granules existing within a particular species of coral. What is still a mystery is why corals need to fluoresce. It is obvious that it is an important condition of their lives, for they feed during the daylight hours and the presence of ultraviolet light, even artificially induced, causes the polyps to expand. I have found that those corals that most often fluoresce live in deep water or in shaded habitats where the sunlight is greatly diminished. However, many of these corals still contain symbiotic algae within their tissues which require light to carry on photosynthesis. It is thought that fluorescence converts ultraviolet radiation to a wavelength that can be used for photosynthesis. The increased light level aids the algae in their food-manufacturing activities. The increase is minimal but perhaps it is just enough to supplement the other rays of the sun, thus providing an adequate supply of oxygen for the coral. What possibly exists is a more efficient use of sunlight within the special conditions of a particular environment. In a multitude of worlds, life seems never to cease exploring the infinite possibilities for its continued existence.

79. Opal Bubble Coral *Plerogyra sinuosa* (Dana) • Mangrove Mussels *Septifer biocularis* (Linnaeus) • Crustose Coralline Algae • 1-1/3 times life size • The Wreck, Bait Grounds Entrance, Ngeruktabel island • 75 feet • 18 June 1971

The animals and plants growing on the wreck are relatively young compared to those living in other areas of the lagoons. The wreck, like a newly formed volcanic island, has been only recently colonized. This young bubble coral is still a single polyp, but eventually it will divide to become a colony. Like the daisy corals, the bubble coral's expanded flesh is much greater than its calyx, enabling the surface of its diaphanous body to trap plankton that drifts into it. In other areas of the lagoons such as Iwayama Bay, the bubble corals live in large colonial masses. During the daylight hours the fleshy bubble-like parts of the tentacles are expanded, probably for protection and also to trap food. At night the "bubbles" partly contract and a thick carpet of the tentacle tips temporarily expands to intensify feeding activity. Unlike the young specimen pictured here, the larger more compact colony must trap large amounts of plankton for its survival.

A heavy concentration of sediment in the water kills some corals. Occasionally, during typhoons when there are tremendous amounts of rain, the soil-laden fresh water run-off destroys corals. Nevertheless, all corals do have some tolerance for sediment and certain ones, such as this bubble variety, have adapted to living in those lagoon areas with greater sediment content. Typhoons are too infrequent to be the major distribution determinant since most corals can withstand an excessive amount of sediment for brief periods of time. It is man's effects on the environment that are often much more disastrous than a typhoon. There is relatively little sediment run-off from the jungle-covered islands but when people cut down the trees or dig soil and rock from the side of Ngemelachel island, the amount of sediment-laden water run-off is increased tremendously and constantly. It is this constant and excessive sediment that kills the corals and other marine life. In their evolutionary adaptation to the environment, corals were not exposed to these conditions and the sudden shift is too drastic, with the result that the animals die.

80. Rooster-comb Oysters *Lopha cristagalli* (Linnaeus) • Crustose Coralline Algae and Red Encrusting Sponge • Life size • Japanese Tanker, Ngederrak lagoon, Ngerchol island • 80 feet • 27 September 1971

Thorny oysters inhabit the underledges of the outer reef, but within the lagoon it is more common to see the ledges and even the wrecks inhabited by rooster-comb oysters. Just as the surfaces of thorny oysters are encrusted with varying sedentary forms of life, the rooster-comb oysters are always host to encrusting sponges. These sponges are often brightly colored and, like the oysters themselves, are plankton feeders.

81. Fairy Nudibranch *Pteraeolidia ianthina* Angas • Rooster-comb Oyster *Lopha*

cristagalli (Linnaeus) • Yellow Tube Corals *Tubastraea coccinea* Lesson • Brown Encrusting Sponge • Twice life size • Bedulyaus point reef, Teongel pass, Ngerchol island • 15 feet • 19 June 1970

The nudibranch, which is a mollusc with no shell, has delicate blue finery which is actually the animal's gills. The structure of the gills greatly increases surface-to-water contact, facilitating the needed gas exchange to sustain life.

The sponge-encrusted rooster-comb oyster, like the nudibranch, is also a mollusc which graphically illustrates the diversity of molluscan life. Like the nudibranch, the rooster-comb oyster has gills but they are enclosed within its bivalved shells. Nudibranchs are able to forego whatever protective shell their ancestors might have had because gradually they acquired a substance within their tissues that has rendered their flesh unappetizing. With their often-conspicuous colors and striking patterns, passing fishes recognize them for what they are—a bad-tasting mouthful.

Obviously, if a nudibranch is unpalatable and predators avoid attacking it, a continuing educational process exists. Consequently, an individual nudibranch or venomous lionfish will occasionally succumb to the gastronomic experiments of predators. A human who values individual existence highly may wonder at the logic of such a process. He may theorize that defenses are useless if either the victim or its attacker is killed, asking, "If the victim is killed despite its venom or bad taste, of what value is its defense to it?" Or, "If the predator dies in the process of feeding, how is it educated?" As always, the answers are complex. Only when we realize that the survival of the species is more important than any one of its members will some of the confusion be cleared away. Venom, unpalatableness, and conspicuous markings are small parts of the incredible genetic heritage of a species constructed over millions of years. If a fish bites into a nudibranch and spits it out again, the nudibranch may die from its injuries but the fish will probably avoid tasting that brightly marked animal in the future. Thus the species, if not always the individual, has a better chance for survival. The same theory would hold true if a predator attacked a lionfish and survived a minor though painful injury. However, a species' survival is not always a matter of "education." If a larger fish tries to eat a lionfish and dies from an injection of venom, the result is one less predator even if the lionfish also dies. It is a matter of numbers. As with plankton, survival is partially insured by abundance. Thus, there is no reason to feel that the single organism need attain a high level of intelligence or education, as we conceive of it, for the species to survive. If, as man believes, the individual has a special importance, it is nothing if not grounded in the whole of life of which intellect or any other single attribute is only a small part.

82. Autumn Ascidians *Polycarpa captiosa* (Sluiter) • Yellow Ascidian *Phallusia julinea* Sluiter • Peppermint Sea Star *Fromia monilis* Perrier • Fluted Oyster *Pycnodonta hyotis* (Linnaeus) • Yellow Tube Corals *Tubastraea coccinea* Lesson • Crustose Coralline Algae, Ascidians and Sponges • Life size • Bedulyaus point reef, Teongel pass, Ngerchol island • 35 feet • 17 August 1971

Most often the marine life on the underledges of the lagoon environments is not as diverse or abundant because there is less tidal flow in many areas. However, under one tremendous coral formation at Bedulyaus point the encrusting life is abundant but consists of different species than those living on the underledges of the outer reefs. This photograph, taken under the fifteen-foot-high coral head at Bedulyaus, shows this distinctive community. The coral head is situated on the outer extremity of the reef top and its underledges are tunneled parallel to the current flowing through Teongel pass. Here, a constant ebb and flow provides these sedentary animals with an abundant supply of plankton.

83. Seen from an altitude of 600 feet is the eastern side of Oreor island and Omekang ridge with some rock islands and a fringing reef in the foreground. The reef is bordered by Towachel Mid pass that separates Oreor from Babeldaob island. Oreor is partly of volcanic origin and partly coral-formed limestone. It is in the limestone islands that marine lakes are formed. To the left and out of sight, Jellyfish Marine Lake is nestled among the ridges of Oreor. Like a slow-motion moment in time, this photograph shows the present-day sea level with the slowly changing reef and island formations. In thousands of years to come, the islands will have altered and the sea level will be elsewhere. The little lagoons of these fringing reefs may one day be transformed into the marine lakes of a future age. (15 October 1971)

84. Anemone Mushroom Coral *Heliofungia actiniformis* (Quoy & Gaimard) • Blue-spotted Cleaner Shrimps *Periclimenes holthuisi* Bruce • Sponges and Algae • 1-2/3 times life size • Kesebekuu pass reef, Mekeald lagoon, Ngeruktabel island • 45 feet • 26 October 1967

Mushroom corals are solitary animals with only one calyx surmounted by a polyp. There are various species that are quite common on the outer reef, the passes, and the lagoons. Most species are primarily nocturnal and their tentacles are usually contracted during the day. This photograph is of a mushroom coral that most often lives in the more secluded areas of the lagoon such as the coves and even in some of the marine lakes. Its tentacles, when expanded, are so large that the coral is often mistaken for a

sea anemone. Cleaner shrimps, which often associate with anemones, are also content to live with this mushroom coral. The shrimps use the coral as a cleaning station and fishes visit them to have their parasites removed. The shrimps also feed upon organisms trapped by their host.

85. Halfbeak *Zenarchopterus dispar* (Cuvier & Valenciennes)? • 1-1/2 times life size • Hera's Cove, Ngelaol, Ngeruktabel island • Surface • 6 June 1970

The greater abundance of life on the outer reefs decreases in variety within the smaller secluded coves where oceanic influence diminishes. Still, this environment is far from a wasteland. Halfbeaks live along the base of the islands where the coral is undercut and vegetation overhangs the water. This male halfbeak is protected from the eyes of birds circling above and swims at the surface eating suspended organic matter and water-striding insects. The halfbeak is counter-shaded—silver below, brown above—and so blends beautifully with the shadows of the rocky shore. Only the brief flash of artificial light used to make this photograph is able to freeze the fish and its reflection against the gently rippling surface.

86. Jellyfish *Mastigias papua* (Lesson) • Jacks *Caranx* sp. • 3/4 life size • Jellyfish Cove II, Risong, Ngeruptachel island • One foot • 28 October 1971

Like giant clams and corals, this jellyfish has symbiotic algae within its bushy manubrium, the area just behind the bell. Sometimes this species also rests on the bottom in the same manner as the *Cassiopaeia* jellyfish with its bell down and its oral surface facing the sun. When on the bottom, its trailing "clubs" droop to the sides permitting a maximum of sunlight to reach the algae for photosynthesis.

In contrast to the more constant bottom-dwelling *Cassiopaeia,* this swimming variety pulses through the water not far below and parallel to the surface. At the same time, it revolves counter-clockwise at the rate of about one revolution per minute with the result that all the symbiotic algae receive an equal exposure to the rays of the sun. Several coves around the islands of Ngederrak lagoon are inhabited by these revolving space stations. The jellyfish are somewhat seasonal and during certain times of the year vacate the coves. Much larger ones live in Ngederrak lagoon and modified types are adapted to living in some of the marine lakes. The larger jellyfish in the coves are often accompanied by a retinue of juvenile jacks that swim with them. The jacks dart in and out of the area behind the bell and urge their host along with nudges on the top of the bell. While swimming, the tiny jacks eat the plankton in the water. During the rainy season, the top four or five inches of the water's surface is fresh-to-brackish in content. Somehow this causes a concentration of tiny copepods and other crustaceans to congregate just below this lighter, less salty layer. As the jellyfish pulses through this concentration of plankton, the jacks busily feast.

87. Maze Coral *Pectinia lactuca* (Pallas) • Life size • Hera's Cove, Ngelaol, Ngeruktabel island • 25 feet • 6 June 1970

I have seen maze coral living in deep water on the outer reef front, in Ulach pass, and in Ngederrak lagoon. Most often it lives either in deeper water or in the shaded environments of the smaller coves.

Maze corals feed at night, so their polyps are contracted during the day. Consequently, the form of the skeleton is easily distinguishable beneath a thin layer of velvet gray flesh. This twisting and turning of form always fascinates me. Though my work is abstracted from nature, I feel the need to capture a certain vibrant quality. Nature provides me with the needed inspiration: within it I sense the dynamic requirements of all living things. Instead of trying to impose an external structure on a particular subject such as this maze coral, I let myself discover the living form within it, and through lighting, camera angle, and framing, which all together determine composition, I hope to create an image that breathes. I would much prefer to watch the graceful swimming movements of a school of fish than look at a photograph of them, unless the image heightens my awareness of the beauty of motion. If a photograph does not evoke a sense of aliveness, it is a poor substitute for one's acutal experience.

88. Macaranga Tree Leaf *Macaranga carolinensis* Volkens • Life size • Jellyfish Cove II, Risong, Ngeruptachel island • Surface • 24 October 1971

A leaf from a Macaranga tree has fallen to the surface of the water and minute aquatic bacteria are hastening its disintegration. It is a very real symbol of a realm where the ocean meets the land, the two interacting in this little cove at the edge of a green jungle.

89. Feather-duster Worm *Sabellastarte indica* (Savigny)? • Grape Algae *Caulerpa racemosa* (Forskal) • Red Encrusting Sponge, Ascidians, and algae • Life size • Jellyfish Cove I, Risong, Ngeruptachel island • 6 feet • 25 June 1971

The many trees of the rock islands completely cover the steeply sloping hills of the coves, even to the edge of the craggy overhang five or six feet above the water. When one of the trees dies, it eventually arcs through the air and plunges into the water. There it rests on an angle with its branches on the bottom and its roots still clinging to the land. Its decomposition is then a matter of many years. In the meantime it becomes a home for other animals such as this tube worm, algae, sponges, ascidians, and multitudes of bacteria and other microscopic organisms that inhabit its surface and interior. Here these creatures will live out their lives and reproduce their kind. In turn, the offspring will find another fallen log on which to live in this world between the sea and land.

Periodically, even the face of an island cracks and falls into the water. Then, little by little, it is covered with a living quilt of many colors. What had been above water is submerged in time and the tiniest creatures build again upon the ancient remains of their ancestors, covering the old skeletons with new life.

90. Fluorescent Bouquet Flower Coral *Lobophyllia hemprichii* (Ehrenberg) • Life size • Hera's Cove, Ngelaol, Ngeruktabel island • 20 feet • 15 June 1970

Fluorescent corals, particularly of the genus *Lobophyllia,* are very common in the coves where they live on the sloping reefs at the base of the islands. The jungle-covered hills often rise almost vertically from their overhanging shores. Consequently, the fringing reefs of these islands receive direct sunlight only part of each day. Many of the corals in these environments of diminished sunlight are fluorescent, which tends to strengthen the theory that irradiation aids survival.

Hera's Cove has a particularly rich concentration of corals along its eastern shore, primarily because the cove is deep, relatively large, and open at both ends. Consequently, the tidal currents can flow through the cove instead of coming to a dead end as they do at Jellyfish Cove I and II. This channel effect in Hera's Cove greatly increases the exchange of fresh ocean water that carries the plankton to the corals and prevents the water in the cove from stagnating.

91. Blackbacked Clownfish *Amphiprion melanopus* Bleeker • Sea Anemone *Pysobrachia douglasi* Kent • False Hammer Oyster *Isognomon isognomon* (Linnaeus) • Twice life size • Ascidian Marine Lake, Mekeald lagoon, Ngeruktabel island • 15 feet • 2 October 1971

At the northeastern end of Ngeruktabel island, a small cove leads from Mekeald lagoon. Along the rocky shore of the cove are two large openings about twenty-five feet apart which are tunnel entrances that lead underground for about 100 feet and connect with a marine lake in Ngeruktabel island. A short walk over a small rise through the jungle brings one to the coral boulder-strewn edge of this small circular body of water. I have named it Ascidian Marine Lake because a fair abundance of these animals live there. Ascidians are like marine lakes in that they are continuous links between two worlds. The ascidians are chordates that live like invertebrates while the marine lakes are links between the ocean and the land. Here the sound of the sea is muted by the surrounding jungle and the shore slopes away gradually at first, then drops steeply into the gloom of the sediment-laden depths. Along its shores are many of the animals that live in the lagoons such as fluorescent and mushroom corals, ascidians, thorny oysters, sponges, and even blackbacked clownfish with their anemones. The tunnels connecting Ascidian Marine Lake with Mekeald lagoon are large and direct.

One gloomy, rainy day I was photographing alone in Ascidian Marine Lake. As I swam along a few feet beneath the surface, I came upon a large floating object. At first it looked like a branch of a palm tree that had fallen into the water because part of it had the serrated look of a palm frond. Then I suddenly realized I was looking at the submerged tail of a crocodile. My eyes quickly followed along the body to the hind legs, the stomach, the fore legs and the head. The head was partly above the water. I couldn't see the animal's eyes. Was he sleeping? I didn't know. Did I dare disturb him? My hands nervously adjusted the controls of my camera as excitement and fear flooded my mind, which seemed severed from my body. Then, half consciously, I realized that my legs were slowly propelling me away from the silently floating form. As the distance between us increased, the crocodile disappeared into the misty gloom. Finally my feet found the bottom near the shore and I slowly stuck my head above water. Thirty feet away the ridge and eyes of the crocodile's head floated on the calm surface of the lake; he knew I was watching him. In the rain, he had come to investigate the disturbance in his lake and found me, just as I found him. As I watched his one eye that watched me, the crocodile silently submerged. Quickly I too submerged, and never taking my eyes from the direction, swam to safety. Halfway back to my base I stopped and looked for the crocodile. He was swimming at the surface along the far shore where the dark green mangrove trees edged the lake.

92. Anemone Mushroom Corals *Heliofungia actiniformis* (Quoy & Gaimard) • Encrusting Algae • Life size • Mushroom Coral Marine Lake, East Cove, Mekeald lagoon, Ngeruktabel island • 5 feet • 11 October 1970

Although all adult mushroom corals are capable of moving slowly about on the reef,

during the initial stages of their lives their skeletons or calices are attached to the bottom. With those mushroom corals living in the lagoons, the calices seem to break off from the bottom at a fairly early stage before the animals attain any appreciable size. However, in the marine lakes the environment is so subdued that the early attached stage of the coral is prolonged. In these quiet waters, the coral polyp is able to expand greatly. This is apparent in the photograph which shows the contrast between the one polyp that is for the moment contracted and the other that is expanded. The absence of a natural predator could make it possible for the mushroom coral polyp to expand greatly in proportion to the size of its calyx. In this same lake I have seen mushroom corals with much larger polyps yet with calices still attached to the bottom. Whatever the particular factors may be, they are no doubt related to the special conditions of the lake.

93. Bracket Fungus Algae *Lobophora variegata* (Lamouroux) • Zebra Nudibranch • Life size • Iwayama Marine Lake, Iwayama Bay, Ngermechaech island • 5 feet • 23 August 1971

Oreor island is shaped roughly like a large U and the body of water that it encloses is called Iwayama Bay. Within this lagoon are quite a number of rock islands among which Ngermechaech is the largest. In the center of Ngermechaech is Iwayama Marine Lake, a large irregular body of deep water. This marine lake is connected to Iwayama Bay by cavernous tunnels that are twenty-five feet below the lake's surface. Unlike Ascidian and Mushroom Coral Marine Lakes, Iwayama Marine Lake is more interior. One must climb up over and down the steep ridge of the island to gain access to the lake. The particular characteristics and the limiting passageways to the different lakes greatly determine the specific plants and animals that live in them. No two lakes are exactly the same and the more interior the lakes the greater the differences between their inhabitants.

It is quite appropriate that this brown-leafed algae is growing in Iwayama Marine Lake. Its broad, rounded leaves are reminiscent of the bracket fungus that grows attached to the massive trunks of ancient trees in the surrounding jungle.

94. Alabaster Sea Cucumber *Opheodesoma* sp. • Red Encrusting Sponge and Brittle Sea Star • Life size • Iwayama Marine Lake, Iwayama Bay, Ngermechaech island • 2 feet • 23 August 1971

With its tentacles extended, this alabaster sea cucumber inches its way like a caterpillar over the trunk of a submerged log, feeding on the tiny organisms while a small brittle sea star clings to its posterior. In the lagoons, these necklacelike sea cucumbers are usually nocturnal and often bear markings of brown, green, and other protective colors that blend with their surroundings. Pure white is a rare color in nature, especially when the animal exists in a non-white environment, which makes this sea cucumber extremely striking, seen against the red sponge and brown log. The animal could be an albino. Its presence in this lake, where there are few predators, may be the reason it has been able to survive. It is in just such situations, through isolation and favorable circumstances, that species diverge to become new species. Here the strange mutations, the wayward tendencies of life, bud and bloom.

95. Autumn Ascidians *Polycarpa captiosa* (Sluiter) • Pink Encrusting Sponge *Spirastrella* sp. • Algae • 1-1/4 times life size • Iwayama Marine Lake, Iwayama Bay, Ngermechaech island • 10 feet • 23 August 1971

Ascidians are often inconspicuous animals and therefore one forgets that they probably inhabit every environment from the outer reefs to the innermost marine lakes. A strange animal, the young ascidian looks like a tiny tadpole that swims freely in the water, moving its body from side to side. Ascidians are actually chordates and therefore are related to vertebrate animals. As free-swimming animals, they have notochords which are simple rod-like structures used for support. This structure is common to vertebrates including man. Nevertheless, as the ascidian grows, it attaches itself to the bottom head-first and "degenerates" into something that resembles a sponge. If we were to compare a butterfly to an ascidian, the butterfly would enclose itself in a cocoon and later emerge as a caterpillar, never to fly again. Given man's set of values, this development on the part of ascidians may seem regressive. If they were capable, ascidians might think that man's ingenious brain has not always preserved him from either natural disasters or those of his own devising and it is possible that these simple animals, with their modest needs, may survive *Homo sapiens*.

96. There are those marine lakes that are still more deeply hidden within the secret jungles of the limestone islands. The umbilical tunnels that connect them with the lagoons are longer and more tortuous and the chances are slim that much new life would enter the lakes through the tunnels. The level of the lake still rises and falls with the change of the tides but the tidal cycle in the lakes is six hours behind that of the lagoon. The water level doesn't begin to rise in the lakes until it is already high tide in the lagoons and, conversely, the level of the water in the lakes only begins to ebb when it is already low tide in the lagoons.

Here at Jellyfish Marine Lake, the land and the trees dominate the little circle of water. The insects hum in rising and falling choruses of conversation and the white jungle birds call to one another. Mangrove trees grow in or near the water; ferns and trees glisten with the dampness of the night's rain. The edge of the lake bottom is laden with the remains of centuries of dead leaves. Heavy rainfall has diluted the salt water and the sweet fragrance of the jungle is stronger than the smell of the sea. (12 November 1970)

97. Sailfin Goby *Gnatholepis puntangoides* (Bleeker) • Brown Mussels *Brachidontes* sp. • Algae • Twice life size • Jellyfish Marine Lake, Omekang ridge, Oreor island • 10 feet • 24 August 1969

Here in Jellyfish Marine Lake, the terrain along the steep incline is reminiscent of a fresh water pond, with fresh water plants and modestly colored fishes like this little goby. The goby perches on the velvety green carpet, raises its dorsal fin, and swivels its keen little eyes looking for any slight movement. Then with a swift lunge, it grabs a mouthful of the mossy plant and swallows the tiny organisms hiding there.

98. Glassy Anemone *Aiptasia pulchella* Carlgren • Brown Mussels *Brachidontes* sp. • Algae • 2-1/2 times life size • Snapper Marine Lake, Ngeremdiu, Ngeruktabel island • 1-1/2 feet • 18 August 1971

Unlike many of the lakes, Snapper Marine Lake is bordered by a grove of very tall mangrove trees of the species *Rhizophora mucronata*. The base of the trees forms a swampy area that is covered by about a foot of water at high tide. At the end of the lake where the water flows underground to the outer lagoon, there is a tiny pass through the mangrove flats. When the water has drained off the mud flats, the remainder flows out through the small stream-like pass. As would be expected, much of the marine life in the lake congregates in this area. Because the lake is bordered by tall trees, its edges are littered with submerged trunks and dead branches. Near the pass, the decaying branches are completely overgrown with a dense layer of algae. There are many sedentary animals that live on these branches, including numerous brown mussels and glassy anemones. The mussels filter the water for food while each transparent anemone traps the plankton with its fragile tentacles.

99. Panchax Goby *Ophiocara* sp. • Mangrove Tree Root, Leaf and Seed Pod Cap

Bruguiera gymnorrhiza (Linnaeus) Lamarck • 1-1/2 times life size • Goby Marine Lake, Ngalap ridge, Oreor island • 5 feet • 25 October 1971

An underwater view of Goby Marine Lake would reveal a world of ethereal beauty. Around the shore, submerged branches of trees are draped with gossamer strands of green algae shimmering in the sunlight while myriad jellyfishes gracefully pulse through the misty water. Hundreds of tiny black-striped gobies hover silently over the angel-hair branches in the green sunlight. Closer to the mangrove-edged shore, the overhanging trees cast shadows that become even darker and deeper among the roots of the mangrove trees. As my eyes become accustomed to the darkness, I see a large goby hovering over a mangrove root. It remains motionless. As I come even closer, the goby suddenly dives into the silt-covered bottom in a cloud of debris and dead leaves.

As seen in this photograph, the juveniles are quite drab, but as they grow to adulthood the yellow color of their posterior dorsal fin as well as anal and caudal fins becomes much more intense and the caudal fin becomes more lyre-shaped like that of some of the fresh water panchaxs'.

This lake is not often visited by man, but it is inhabited by at least one large fish. The gobies must be on their guard. However, man is a stranger to them and if he remains motionless, as I continued to do, the frightened little goby soon reappears. In fact, it even brings its friends which emerge from the shadows in droves. Before long I was surrounded by dozens of curiosity seekers. For me these are always moments of joy; through them I have discovered that there are still places on earth where I evoke more curiosity than fear.

100. Mangrove Snapper *Lutjanus argentimaculatus* (Forskål) • Decaying Mangrove Tree Leaves *Rhizophora mucronata* Lamarck • 1/2 life size • Snapper Marine Lake, Ngeremdiu, Ngeruktabel island • 5 feet • 20 July 1971

The most abundant fishes in Snapper Marine Lake are the snappers, of which there are at least two different species, the most common of which is the mangrove snapper. Normally, mangrove snappers, as their name implies, live in mangrove swamps and brackish water areas as well as in rivers long distances from the ocean. Consequently, it is not surprising that these snappers inhabit some of the more interior marine lakes where the water is brackish and the bottom is littered with decaying leaves instead of growing corals.

These snappers are equipped with a pair of needle-sharp canine teeth with which they grasp their prey. However, I am not quite certain what they eat in the lake which also contains a group of larger ox-eye tarpon, as well as smaller archer fish, *Monodactylus,* and other smaller fishes. The most obvious source of food is the mussels which grow everywhere. When the shell is cracked and the bivalve is offered to the snappers, it is avidly devoured. The snapper manages to separate the flesh from the still-attached shells and swallow it. Even if the shells were not cracked, they are quite fragile and could be crushed easily between the snapper's toothed jaws.

Like many of the reef fishes, the varying coloration of the mangrove snapper is similar to that of its environment, changing from golden brown to rust red. Often these fish hide under the submerged limbs of the decaying trees and, in the shadows cast by the branches, blend with the mangrove swamp world.

101. Mangrove Tree Leaves and Seed Pod Cap *Bruguiera gymnorrhiza* (Linnaeus) Lamarck • 1-1/3 times life size • Goby Marine Lake, Ngalap ridge, Oreor island • 6 feet • 25 October 1971

In the watery world of the marine lakes, growth and decay are equally colorful. In their golden autumn hues, these mangrove leaves display one last blush of life as they are consumed by countless bacteria. When the flow is stilled in the many rivers and tributaries of their veins, their substance is returned to the earth by the living. Even the seed pod cap, having completed its function in the reproductive cycle, is returned to the elements. Like the crown of the little prince gone off to another star, it lies discarded—golden in decay.

When I see how nature lives and dies, I wonder at the agonies invented by man. How much healthier to live as a leaf lives and die as a leaf falls...a small part of the whole.

102. Flame Ascidians *Polycarpa simplex* Tokioka • Algae • 1-1/4 times life size • Jellyfish Marine Lake, Omekang ridge, Oreor island • 4 feet • 31 August 1969

The shallow rim of Jellyfish Marine Lake abounds in deep green algae. Here and there, little clustered communities of ascidians are attached. When a mangrove tree shades the animals from the sun, they blend in the darkness with the algae and submerged mangrove roots. However, the earth is never still, and as it turns the sunlight moves from leaf to leaf, stealing down across the darkened world below. As the sunlight suffuses the ascidians, they glow and suddenly burst into flame.

103. Ox-eye Tarpon *Megalops cyprinoides* (Broussonet) • Life size • Goby Marine

Lake, Ngalap ridge, Oreor island • 3 feet • 21 October 1971

One dark rainy day I was swimming in Goby Marine Lake. Suddenly, tiny liquid projectiles pierced the surface of the lake in explosions of air and water that danced and boiled with the mingled forces of salt water and fresh water, warm and cold. The silence was filled with a million muted detonations. The rain was cold; I was glad to be underwater where it was warmer and continued swimming. After a time, the rain slowed to a whisper. I glided silently through milky layers of sediment interspersed with clearer layers. The bottom was somewhere below and I felt like an aviator slipping through clouds far above the unseen earth. As I glided along, half dreaming, another dreamer with large, sleepy eyes emerged out of the mist. I stopped breathing and raised my camera. The silvery fish glided closer, still in reverie, but the flash that recorded his image rudely awakened him. The tarpon turned and zig-zagged away, disappearing into the mist. Only my memories and this photograph remain.

My words create a mood of mist and sky but the photograph evokes a different experience, transporting me to a world of perpetual darkness. It is like an archetypal image of the abyss where one turns a midnight corner and suddenly encounters this creature, Life—shimmering in platinum and gold.

104. Mangrove Mussels *Septifer bilocularis* Linnaeus • Red and Yellow Encrusting Sponges • Life size • Goby Marine Lake, Ngalap ridge, Oreor island • 5 feet • 21 October 1971

Although the marine lakes are not as dark as the abyss or as the nether reaches of one's imagination, they do have secret places where trees root in the mud. Here the mangroves stand, while their submerged roots provide support for other creatures.

105. Flacourtia Tree *Flacourtia rukam* Z. & M. • Mangrove Tree *Bruguiera gymnorrhiza* (Linnaeus) Lamarck • 1/3 life size • Snapper Marine Lake, Ngeremdiu, Ngeruktabel island • 20 July 1971

The surface of the water mirrors sunlight and shadow alike. Though the trees are rooted in the earth, their green leaves are designed for the sun...rooted in the sky, each sharing the sunlight.

106. Bird's Nest Fern *Asplenium nidus* Linnaeus • Hare's Foot Fern *Davallia solida* (Forst.) Sw. • 2/3 life size • Snapper Marine Lake, Ngermdiu, Ngeruktabel island • 15 September 1971

As I photographed this exquisite pattern formed by one fern overshadowing another, I was entranced with light and dark and all the green loveliness of the colors. I was surrounded by the silence of the jungle and the rays of sunlight slanting through the branches of the trees. For a moment, I was again aware of something more than all the elements and I experienced a conjunction of forces that finds its expression in this photograph. I sat there in the mud, not merely an observer but also a participant... a unique emanation from the ooze. While I photographed, the earth turned and the light changed, grew dim and finally disappeared behind the trees and the high ridge surrounding the lake. I trembled with a kind of ecstasy mingled with the slightest fear. The experience was real but I knew the photograph, like a child, had still to be born. Like a parent, I was nervous with anticipation. Now, as I look at this photograph and think back, a sadness comes over me. Sometimes I think it would have been better had I never tried to capture the image. In so doing, I have tried to hold it forever and somehow have lost it. The experience is in the photograph. As a child, I never photographed. Experiences flowed through me and somehow stayed. I did not try to capture them and they are always young within me. I'm not sad if, one by one, they slip from my memory. They go and I don't miss them, for around me life is still young and green. But the photographs are my children. They are moments preserved that someday must fade and die. In my healthiest moments, I know that nothing should ever be fixed. To expect more is to court sadness. Someday, I hope my images will flow through me as they do at their conception, when I am always happiest.

107. Jellyfish *Mastigias papua* (Lesson) • 2/3 life size • Jellyfish Marine Lake, Omekang ridge, Oreor island • 3 feet • 24 August 1969

This *Mastigias* jellyfish is the biologically modified version of the one living in the coves. In this marine lake there is no need for large stinging clubs for defense or feeding. The jellyfish have adapted to the particular conditions of their world. The lake contains literally thousands and thousands of these inner space travelers, pulsating through a clear plasma of the living earth.

While this photograph illustrates the past mutability of life, it also symbolizes the next moment of existence. The sun shines down upon us, filling our flesh with warmth and our spirits with joy. Only if we are aware do we see its rays shimmering through the substance of our lives, splitting like chromosomes in a millionth moment of creation...a creation without beginning or end. When I see that which we call death, I ask myself, "what is death?"...merely a rearrangement of form. I cannot find this "death" of which man speaks. I see only life.

NGEAUR

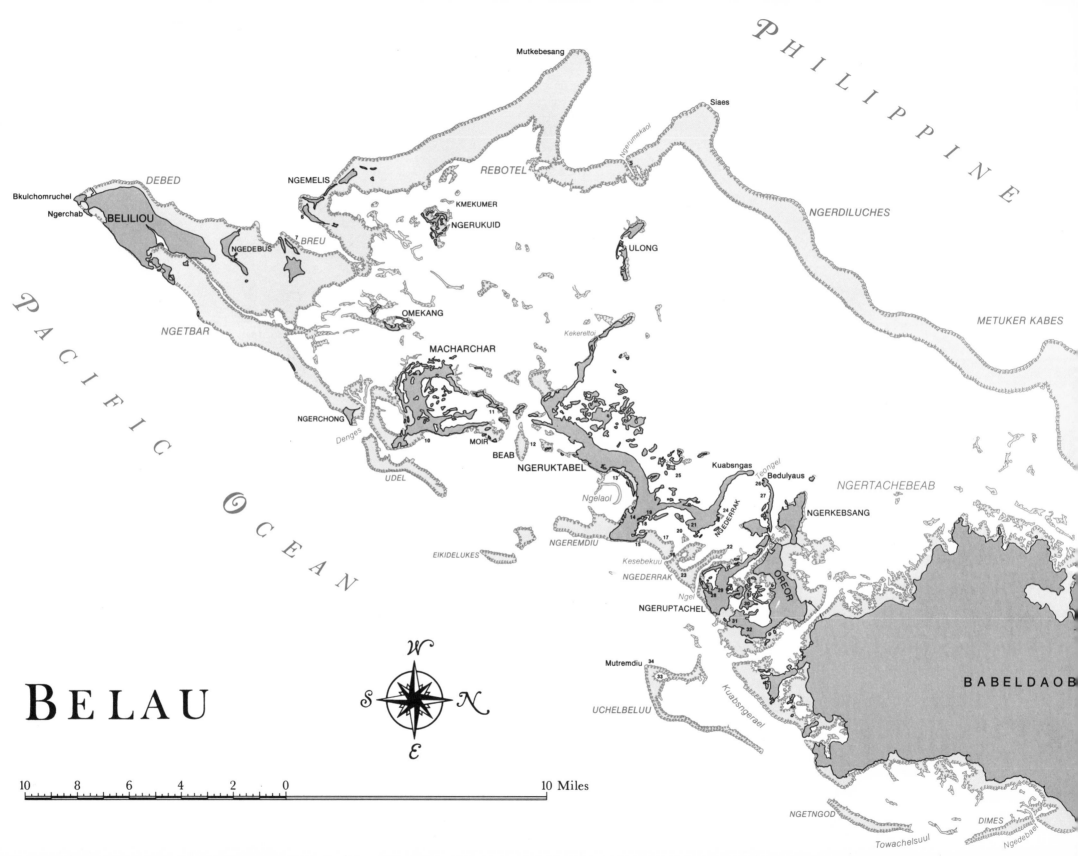

PHILIPPINE

Mutkebesang

Siaes

DEBED

REBOTEL

NGERDILUCHES

Bkulchomruchel

BELILIOU

NGEMELIS

KMEKUMER

NGERUKUID

METUKER KABES

Ngerchab

BREU

NGEDEBUS

ULONG

NGETBAR

OMEKANG

Kekereltoi

MACHARCHAR

NGERCHONG

Denges

MOIR

BEAB

NGERUKTABEL

Kuabsngas

Bedulyaus

NGERTACHEBEAB

UDEL

Ngelaol

NGEDERRAK

NGERKEBSANG

EIKIDELUKES

NGEREMDIU

Kesebekuu

OREOR

NGEDERRAK

Ngei

NGERUPTACHEL

BABELDAOB

Mutremdiu

BELAU

UCHELBELUU

Kuabsngerael

NGETNGOD

DIMES

Towachelsuul

Ngedebael

10   8   6   4   2   0   10 Miles

This map of Belau, or Palau as it is known to many non-Belauans, illustrates the multitude of islands and reefs of this complex environment and shows all the diving locations where the photographs for this book were made. Only Belau names are used on this map. They are differentiated by varying type faces to show the islands, reefs, passes, points, lagoons, and coves. In my own diving locations (designated by numbers on the map), I use non-Belauan names such as "The Great Reef," "patch reef," or "Babeldaob island." The people of Belau have specific names for places which comprise an island or group of islands, though more often a name has been given to only a particular location. Babeldaob means "upper ocean" and Uchelbeluu means "the beginning of beluu (land)."

The reader will not find Belauan names on any other maps or nautical charts of these islands, simply because the people of Belau did not have a part in making them. This fragment of land is theirs, however, and it seems only appropriate that I use their place names in this book. I do this out of respect for the people of Belau—that they may have pride in their language and that these names may be preserved.

1 PASS REEF, NGERUANGEL REEF

2 ULACH PASS, NGCHEANGEL ISLANDS

3 SOUTHWEST WALL, NGCHEANGEL ISLANDS

4 NGERUTECHETACHEL REEF, TOWACHELMLENGUI PASS, BABELDAOB ISLAND

5 NGERUMEKAOL PASS, ULONG ISLAND

6 THE GREAT REEF, BAILECHESENGEL ISLAND, NGEMELIS ISLANDS

7 BREU REEF, NGERCHEU ISLAND

8 WEST WALL, BLACK BEACH, NGEAUR ISLAND

9 SOUTHWEST WALL, CANTIN REEF, NGEAUR ISLAND

10 EAST REEF, MACHARCHAR ISLANDS

11 FRINGING REEF, MACHARCHAR LAGOON, NGCHELOBEL ISLAND

12 BEAB PASS REEF, BEAB ISLAND

13 HERA'S COVE, NGELAOL, NGERUKTABEL ISLAND

14 SNAPPER MARINE LAKE, NGEREMDIU, NGERUKTABEL ISLAND

15 NGEREMDIU REEF, WHITE CLIFF, NGERUKTABEL ISLAND

16 KESEBEKUU PASS REEF, KESEBEKUU PASS

17 KESEBEKUU PASS REEF, MEKEALD LAGOON, NGERUKTABEL ISLAND

18 EAST COVE REEF, MEKEALD LAGOON, NGERUKTABEL ISLAND

19 MUSHROOM CORAL MARINE LAKE, EAST COVE, MEKEALD LAGOON, NGERUKTABEL ISLAND

20 PATCH REEF, MEKEALD LAGOON, NGERUKTABEL ISLAND

21 ASCIDIAN MARINE LAKE, MEKEALD LAGOON, NGERUKTABEL ISLAND

22 PATCH REEF, NGEL PASS, NGEDERRAK LAGOON

23 NGEDERRAK REEF, NGEDERRAK LAGOON

24 PATCH REEF, NGEDERRAK LAGOON, NGERUKTABEL ISLAND

25 THE WRECK, BAIT GROUNDS ENTRANCE, NGERUKTABEL ISLAND

26 BEDULYAUS POINT REEF, TEONGEL PASS, NGERCHOL ISLAND

27 JAPANESE TANKER, NGEDERRAK LAGOON, NGERCHOL ISLAND

28 JELLYFISH COVE I, RISONG, NGERUPTACHEL ISLAND

29 JELLYFISH COVE II, RISONG, NGERUPTACHEL ISLAND

30 IWAYAMA MARINE LAKE, IWAYAMA BAY, NGERMECHAECH ISLAND

31 GOBY MARINE LAKE, NGALAP RIDGE, OREOR ISLAND

32 JELLYFISH MARINE LAKE, OMEKANG RIDGE, OREOR ISLAND

33 MUTREMDIU POINT LAGOON, UCHELBELUU REEF

34 MUTREMDIU POINT, UCHELBELUU REEF

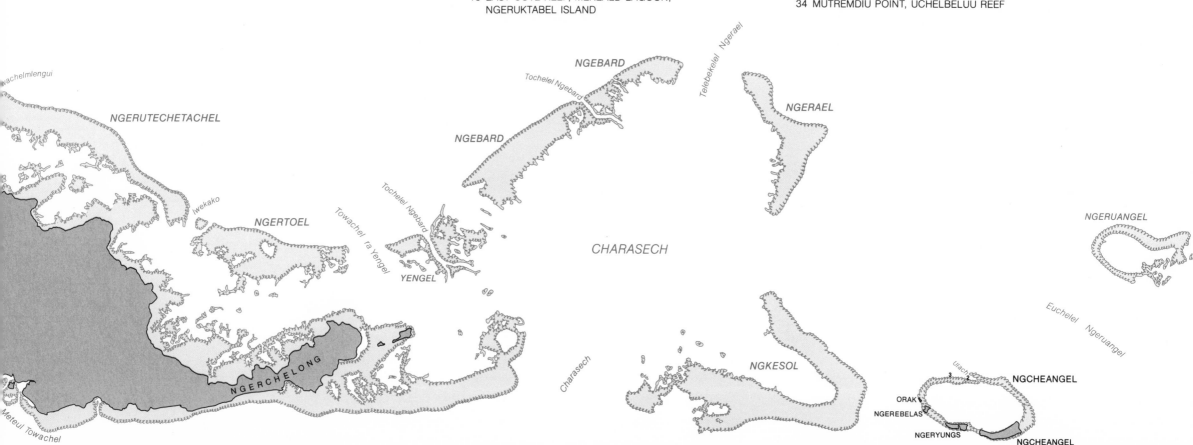

Dedication

Merkemiu

ar chad era Belau

lobengkel a mui el beltik el reng

ma klou el deureng el kirel tial klebokl Belau

⟙ ⟙ ⟙

For

the people of Belau

with love and affection

and with great appreciation for the beauty that is Belau

Acknowledgments

Nothing is nurtured in a vacuum or fulfilled in isolation, especially works of art.
All living creatures, including artists, are part of larger webs of experiences and relationships
that together contribute to what eventually blooms. These photographs are
not the result of my efforts alone and this book would not exist without much help from:
Tucker Abbott, Emiliano Adelbai, Haruo Adelbai, Taro Alexander, Gerald Allen, Cesare Antoniacci,
Frank Arcara, James Atz, Kikutaro Baba, Isaac Bai, Edward Barnard, Frederick Bayer,
Robert Bear, Joseph Behar, Patricia Bergquist, Uldekel and Ermang Besebs, Tewid Boisek,
Nathan Brill, Earl Broady, Patrick Bryan, Warren Burgess, Fenner Chase, Thomas Chilton, Jack Cobb,
Bruce Collette, Vernon Cooper, Lon Cottingham, E. E. Cummings, Charles Cutress, Arthur Dahl,
Yecheluu Dimas, Nina Dlutaoch, Maxwell Doty, Maureen Downey, Don Duffy, Loren Eiseley,
Lucius Eldredge, William Emerson, Thomas Ermang, Alice Faulkner, Sally Faulkner, Duncan Fitchet,
Will Gallagher, Thomas Gibson, Charles Golding, Ernst Haas, Willard Hartman, Eva Hawkins,
Richard Hoar, Frederick Horbert, Harvey Horowitz, Henry Horowitz, Carol Howard, James Kinto,
Idesmang Kitalong, Hirao Kloulchad, Leslie Knapp, Singer Kochi, Edward Leczek, Eckart Leistikow,
Gerard Leprine, Milton Liberty, Kenneth Lieberman, Isadore Lipson, Becky Madraisau, Michael Martin,
James McVey, Hiob Mesubed, John Michel, Doug Mitchell, Francoise Monniot, Francisco Morei,
Sakie Morriss, John Moylan, Elliott and Phyllis Nagelberg, Fred Nathan, George Ngirarsaol,
Erica Ngirausui, Yaoch Ngirmang, Thomas O'Brien, William Old, Jonas Olekeriil, Dennis Opresko,
Demei Otobed, Robert and Hera Owen, Larry Pardue, Toshiro Paulis, David Pawson, Frank Pecca,
John Prescott, John Randall, Richard Randall, Sidney Rapoport, Kenneth Read, Peter Ritner,
Ronald Rittenhouse, Martin Rosenthal, Belhaim Sakuma, Sandra Sharp, C. Lavett Smith,
Michael Sonino, Gale Sphon, Sam Spinelli, David Stone, Yosiharu Sungino, Takeshi Suzuki,
Ted and Mae Tansy, Takasi Tokioka, Yosinao Ubedei, David Vitarelli, William and Henrietta Vitarelli,
Sonia Wedge, Fred Weitz, John Wells, Peter and Ann Wilson, Robert Woodward, Saztki Yobech

Concept and Design by Douglas Faulkner

Typographic Design by Don Duffy

Map created by R. R. Donnelley Cartographic
Services under the direction of Duncan Fitchet.
Design by Will Gallagher

Printed in Six-color "Stonetone" by Rapoport Printing Corp.,
New York, New York

Photo typography by The Composition Shop, Inc.,
New York, New York

Bound by A. Horowitz & Son • Bookbinders,
Clifton, New Jersey